most loved recipe collection most loved recipe collection most loved recipe collection m
most loved recipe collection most loved recipe collection most loved recipe collection most lo
most loved recipe collection most loved recipe collection most loved recipe collec
most loved recipe collection most loved recipe collection most loved recipe collection
most loved recipe collection most loved recipe collection  collection
most loved recipe collection most loved recipe collec most loved recipe collecti
most loved recipe collection most loved recipe collection most loved recipe collection n
collection most loved recipe collection most loved recipe most loved ed recipe
most loved recipe collection most loved recipe collection most loved recipe collec
most loved recipe collection most loved recipe collection most loved recipe collection m
most loved recipe collection most loved recipe collection most loved recipe collection most lo
most loved recipe collection most loved recipe collection most loved recipe collection most lo
most loved recipe collection most loved recipe collection most loved recipe collection
most loved recipe collection most loved recipe collection most loved recipe collecti
most loved recipe collection most loved recipe collection most loved recipe collection m
collection most loved recipe collection most loved recipe collection most loved recipe
most loved recipe collection most loved recipe collection most loved recipe collec
most loved recipe collection most loved recipe collection most loved recipe collection m
most loved recipe collection most loved recipe collection most loved recipe collection most lo
most loved recipe collection most loved recipe collection most loved recipe collecti
most loved recipe collection most loved recipe collection most loved recipe collection
most loved recipe collection most loved recipe collection most loved recipe collection
most loved recipe collection most loved recipe collection most loved recipe collect
most loved recipe collection most loved recipe collection most loved recipe collection
collection most loved recipe collection most loved recipe collection most loved recipe
most loved recipe collection most loved recipe collection most loved recipe collec
most loved recipe collection most loved recipe collection most loved recipe collection n
most loved recipe collection most loved recipe collection most loved recipe collection most lo
most loved recipe collection most loved recipe collection most loved recipe collec
most loved recipe collection most loved recipe collection most loved recipe collection
most loved recipe collection most loved recipe collection most loved recipe collect
most loved recipe collection most loved recipe collection most loved recipe collection n
most loved recipe collection most loved recipe collection most loved recipe collection
collection most loved recipe collection most loved recipe collection most loved recipe

most
loved
pies

Pictured on front cover:
Apple Pie and Favourite Pie Crust, page 42

Pictured on back cover:
Salmon Pie, page 96; Curry Tuna Quiche, page 98

Most Loved Pies
Copyright © Company's Coming Publishing Limited

First Printing August 2009

Library and Archives Canada Cataloguing in Publication
Paré, Jean, date
Most loved pies / Jean Paré.
(Most loved recipe collection)
Includes indexes.
ISBN 978-1-897069-69-1
1. Pies. I. Title. II. Series: Paré, Jean, date- . Most loved recipe collections.
TX773.P359095 2009   641.8'652   C2008-907285-5

Published by
Company's Coming Publishing Limited
2311 – 96 Street
Edmonton, Alberta, Canada T6N 1G3
Tel: 780-450-6223   Fax: 780-450-1857
www.companyscoming.com

Company's Coming is a registered trademark owned by
Company's Coming Publishing Limited

We acknowledge the financial support of the Government of Canada through the Book Publishing Industry Development Program (BPIDP) for our publishing activities.

Printed in China

We gratefully acknowledge the following suppliers for their generous support of our Test and Photography Kitchens:

Broil King Barbecues
Corelle®
Hamilton Beach® Canada
Lagostina®
Proctor Silex® Canada
Tupperware®

Our special thanks to the following businesses for providing props for photography:

Anchor Hocking Canada
Baker's Secret
Brown & Co. Ltd.
Canhome Global
Casa Bugatti
Cherison Enterprises Inc.
Chintz & Company
Clays Handmade Ceramic
Creations by Design
Danesco Inc.
Dansk Gifts
Eaton's
Enchanted Kitchen
Exquisite Sewing Centre
Island Pottery Inc.
Klass Works
La Cache
LeGnome
Linens 'N Things
Michaels
Mikasa Home Store
Mugsie's Coffee House
Mystique Pottery & Gifts

Pfaltzgraff Canada
Pier 1 Imports
Salisbury Greenhouse & Landscaping
Scona Clayworks
Stokes
Stor-Age Revolution Inc.
The Basket House
The Bay
The Bombay Company
The Glasshouse
The Royal Doulton Store
Tile & Stone
Totally Bamboo
Tupperware
Wicker World
Winners Stores

Pictured from left: Cheesecake Pie, page 30; Pepper And Ham Quiche and Shrimp Quiche, page 92; Strawberry Cheese Tarts and Frozen Yogurt Tarts, page 110; Rich Chocolate Tart, page 76, Almond Rhubarb Tart, page 74, and Peach And Almond Tart, page 75

table of contents

"Never share a recipe you wouldn't use yourself."

the Company's Coming story

Jean Paré (pronounced "jeen PAIR-ee") grew up understanding that the combination of family, friends and home cooking is the best recipe for a good life. From her mother, she learned to appreciate good cooking, while her father praised even her earliest attempts in the kitchen. When Jean left home, she took with her a love of cooking, many family recipes and an intriguing desire to read cookbooks as if they were novels!

When her four children had all reached school age, Jean volunteered to cater the 50th anniversary celebration of the Vermilion School of Agriculture, now Lakeland College, in Alberta, Canada. Working out of her home, Jean prepared a dinner for more than 1,000 people, launching a flourishing catering operation that continued for over 18 years. During that time, she had countless opportunities to test new ideas with immediate feedback—resulting in empty plates and contented customers! Whether preparing cocktail sandwiches for a house party or serving a hot meal for 1,500 people, Jean Paré earned a reputation for great food, courteous service and reasonable prices.

As requests for her recipes increased, Jean was often asked the question, "Why don't you write a cookbook?" Jean responded by teaming up with her son, Grant Lovig, in the fall of 1980 to form Company's Coming Publishing Limited. The publication of *150 Delicious Squares* on April 14, 1981 marked the debut of what would soon become one of the world's most popular cookbook series.

The company has grown since those early days when Jean worked from a spare bedroom in her home. Today, she continues to write recipes while working closely with the staff of the Recipe Factory, as the Company's Coming test kitchen is affectionately known. There she fills the role of mentor, assisting with the development of recipes people most want to use for everyday cooking and easy entertaining. Every Company's Coming recipe is kitchen-tested before it is approved for publication.

Jean's daughter, Gail Lovig, is responsible for marketing and distribution, leading a team that includes sales personnel located in major cities across Canada. Company's Coming cookbooks are distributed in Canada, the United States, Australia and other world markets. Bestsellers many times over in English, Company's Coming cookbooks have also been published in French and Spanish.

Familiar and trusted in home kitchens around the world, Company's Coming cookbooks are offered in a variety of formats. Highly regarded as kitchen workbooks, the softcover Original Series, with its lay-flat plastic comb binding, is still a favourite among readers.

Jean Paré's approach to cooking has always called for quick and easy recipes using everyday ingredients. That view has served her well. The recipient of many awards, including the Queen Elizabeth Golden Jubilee Medal, Jean was appointed Member of the Order of Canada, her country's highest lifetime achievement honour.

Jean continues to gain new supporters by adhering to what she calls The Golden Rule of Cooking: *Never share a recipe you wouldn't use yourself.* It's an approach that has worked—millions of times over!

foreword

What's not to love about pie? Just try to eat a slice without feeling the goodness all the way down to your toes! For many of us, pie invokes special memories—the taste of berry pie with ice cream brings back moments from past summers, while a hot meat pie conjures up holiday meals spent with family and friends.

Most Loved Pies makes it easy to pull the ultimate comfort food from your oven (or freezer!) any time. This collection of recipes not only includes tempting twists on old favourites, but also tried-and-true classics like lemon meringue, pumpkin and of course, apple pie.

Fruit pies are marvellous baked with fresh pickings, but you can also stock your freezer and enjoy these pies year-round. Cream pies make luscious after-dinner treats, and frozen pies are great finales for backyard barbecues. For a coffee-time snack, try a rich, nutty pie. Sweet and savoury tarts fit neatly in the hand while packing a mouthful of flavour—perfect as appetizers. And don't forget about hearty, savoury pies to serve up as delicious main courses.

Pies are often associated with hours of work, but pie-making doesn't have to be difficult. *Most Loved Pies* includes time-saving hints and sidebars outlining everything from foolproof pastry to pie-perfect baking methods. You can use shortcuts like ready-made pastry, but homemade crust can be economical, easy and fun too! Get started with our basic pastry recipe on page 42.

It's important for the bottom crust to bake evenly, so pies should be baked on the bottom rack. If you're baking a two-crust pie, it's helpful to use a glass pie plate because you can see the bottom crust through the glass and ensure that it's nicely browned and thoroughly baked. Fruit pies keep in the freezer (except those made with custard) for three to six months; they can be frozen baked or unbaked, but unbaked ones should be put into the oven frozen, not thawed. Frozen dessert pies will freeze well for up to three months, but cream and custard pies are best served freshly made.

A wonderful complement to any setting or season, pie is especially versatile. Serve one up piping hot on a chilly autumn night or as a cool, creamy spring treat. No matter what the occasion—bake sale, party or family gathering—*Most Loved Pies* has a perfect pie recipe to match.

Jean Paré

nutrition information

Each recipe is analyzed using the most current version of the Canadian Nutrient File from Health Canada, which is based on the United States Department of Agriculture (USDA) Nutrient Database.

- If more than one ingredient is listed (such as "butter or hard margarine"), or if a range is given (1 – 2 tsp., 5 – 10 mL), only the first ingredient or first amount is analyzed.

- For meat, poultry and fish, the serving size per person is based on the recommended 4 oz. (113 g) uncooked weight (without bone), which is 2 – 3 oz. (57 – 85 g) cooked weight (without bone)—approximately the size of a deck of playing cards.

- Milk used is 1% M.F. (milk fat), unless otherwise stated.

- Cooking oil used is canola oil, unless otherwise stated.

- Ingredients indicating "sprinkle," "optional," or "for garnish" are not included in the nutrition information.

- The fat in recipes and combination foods can vary greatly depending on the sources and types of fats used in each specific ingredient. For these reasons, the amount of saturated, monounsaturated and polyunsaturated fats may not add up to the total fat content.

Vera C. Mazurak, Ph.D.
Nutritionist

This recipe has a chocolate topping over the ice cream—try it with hot Deluxe Chocolate Sauce, below, for the best Mud Pie ever. Garnish with shaved chocolate baking squares and toasted sliced almonds.

deluxe chocolate sauce

A real treat to have on hand. Store remaining sauce in airtight container in refrigerator for up to one week or in freezer for up to one month.

Semi-sweet chocolate chips	2 cups	500 mL
Butter (or hard margarine)	1/2 cup	125 mL
Instant coffee granules	1 tbsp.	15 mL
Vanilla extract	1 tbsp.	15 mL
Salt	1/8 tsp.	0.5 mL
Icing (confectioner's) sugar	2 cups	500 mL
Golden corn syrup	1 cup	250 mL
Hot water	1 cup	250 mL

Combine first 5 ingredients in small saucepan. Heat and stir on medium until melted and smooth. Remove from heat.

Add next 3 ingredients. Beat until smooth. Makes 4 1/2 cups (1.1 L).

2 tbsp. (30 mL) chocolate sauce:
118 Calories; 5.3 g Total Fat (1.6 g Mono, 0.2 g Poly, 3.2 g Sat); 7 mg Cholesterol; 19 g Carbohydrate; 1 g Fibre; trace Protein; 40 mg Sodium

Mud Pie *A Classic!*

CRUST		
Butter (or hard margarine)	1/2 cup	125 mL
Chocolate wafer crumbs	2 cups	500 mL

FILLING		
Coffee ice cream, softened (see Note)	4 cups	1 L

CHOCOLATE TOPPING		
Granulated sugar	2/3 cup	150 mL
Cocoa, sifted if lumpy	1/3 cup	75 mL
Whipping cream	1/3 cup	75 mL
Butter (or hard margarine)	3 tbsp.	50 mL
Vanilla extract	1 tsp.	5 mL

WHIPPED CREAM		
Whipping cream (see Tip, page 22)	1 cup	250 mL
Granulated sugar	1 tbsp.	15 mL
Vanilla extract	1/2 tsp.	2 mL

Crust: Melt butter in medium saucepan. Remove from heat. Add wafer crumbs. Stir well. Press firmly in bottom and up side of 9 inch (22 cm) pie plate. Bake in 350°F (175°C) oven for 10 minutes. Let stand on wire rack to cool.

Filling: Spread ice cream in crust. Freeze until firm.

Chocolate Topping: Measure all 5 ingredients into small saucepan. Heat and stir on medium until mixture comes to a boil. Remove from heat. Cool for 10 minutes. Spread over ice cream filling. Freeze.

Whipped Cream: Beat all 3 ingredients in medium bowl until soft peaks form. Spread over pie. Cuts into 8 wedges.

1 wedge: 752 Calories; 52.6 g Total Fat (9.7 g Mono, 2.3 g Poly, 31.2 g Sat); 216 mg Cholesterol; 63 g Carbohydrate; 2 g Fibre; 8 g Protein; 358 mg Sodium

Pictured at right.

Note: If coffee ice cream isn't available, dissolve 1 tbsp. (15 mL) instant coffee granules in 2 tbsp. (30 mL) hot water. Mix into same amount of softened vanilla ice cream.

Layered Fudge Frost

CHOCOLATE SAUCE

Evaporated milk (or half-and-half cream)	1 cup	250 mL
Semi-sweet chocolate chips	1 cup	250 mL
Miniature marshmallows	1 cup	250 mL

FILLING

Vanilla ice cream, softened	4 cups	1 L
Baked 9 inch (22 cm) pie shell (see Tip, page 18)	1	1
Chopped pecans (or walnuts)	2 tbsp.	30 mL

A super pie—vanilla ice cream is layered with just the right amount of chocolate. Easy to cut while frozen.

tip

Dip your knife in hot water before cutting frozen desserts.

Chocolate Sauce: Heat evaporated milk and chocolate chips in small saucepan on medium-low, stirring often until chips start to melt. Add marshmallows. Heat and stir until melted. Cool.

Filling: Spread half of ice cream in pie shell. Freeze for 45 minutes. Spread half of chocolate sauce over ice cream. Freeze for 60 minutes. Repeat with remaining ice cream and chocolate sauce.

Sprinkle with pecans. Freeze. Cuts into 8 wedges.

1 wedge: 527 Calories; 33.0 g Total Fat (5.8 g Mono, 1.3 g Poly, 18.1 g Sat); 130 mg Cholesterol; 51 g Carbohydrate; 2 g Fibre; 9 g Protein; 209 mg Sodium

Pictured below.

Left: Layered Fudge Frost, this page
Right: Mud Pie, page 6

The perfect treat for the peanut butter lover.

making chocolate curls

- Begin with a block of good quality chocolate (couverture makes the glossiest curls).

- To curl properly, the chocolate should be neither too cold nor too warm. Start with chocolate at room temperature (72° F, 22° C).

- Soften chocolate slightly by placing it in a cloth or paper towel and holding it in your hands for a few minutes; alternatively, place it under the bulb of a lamp or in the microwave for 3 seconds at a time (high power) a few times until it is just slightly soft.

- Once it has reach the right consistency, hold the chocolate block in some toweling to keep the heat of your hand from melting it while you make the curls.

- Using a sharp paring knife, vegetable peeler or melon baller, start from the top of the block and work your way down at a 45 degree angle. Light pressure creates tighter curls whereas heavier pressure creates larger, more open curls.

- If the chocolate splinters, warm it for a few more minutes.

- If you just get straight strips, try curling them by hand.

- Use a skewer or other utensil to lift the curls up and onto the pie.

Frozen Peanut Butter Pie

CRUST

Butter (or hard margarine)	1/3 cup	75 mL
Chocolate wafer crumbs	1 1/4 cups	300 mL
Ground (or finely chopped) peanuts	1/3 cup	75 mL
Granulated sugar	1/4 cup	60 mL

FILLING

Egg whites (large), room temperature	2	2
Granulated sugar	1/2 cup	125 mL
Egg yolks (large)	2	2
Cream cheese, softened	8 oz.	250 g
Granulated sugar	1/4 cup	60 mL
Creamy peanut butter	1 cup	250 mL
Vanilla extract	1 tsp.	5 mL
Whipping cream (see Tip, page 22)	1 cup	250 mL
Granulated sugar	2 tsp.	10 mL
Vanilla	1/2 tsp.	2 mL
Ground or (finely chopped) peanuts	2 tbsp.	30 mL
Chocolate curls, for garnish	2 tbsp.	30 mL

Crust: Melt butter in medium saucepan. Remove from heat. Add next 3 ingredients. Stir well. Press in bottom and up side of 9 inch (22 cm) pie plate. Bake in 350°F (175°C) oven for 10 minutes. Let stand on wire rack to cool.

Filling: Beat egg whites in small bowl until soft peaks form. Add sugar, 1 tbsp. (15 mL) at a time, beating constantly until stiff peaks form and sugar is dissolved.

Using same beaters, beat next 3 ingredients in medium bowl until smooth. Add peanut butter and vanilla. Beat well. Mixture will be quite stiff. Fold in egg white mixture.

Beat next 3 ingredients in small bowl until stiff peaks form. Fold into peanut butter mixture. Spread in crust.

Sprinkle with peanuts and chocolate. Freeze. Let stand at room temperature for about 35 minutes before cutting.

Cuts into 8 wedges.

(continued on next page)

1 wedge: 695 Calories; 52.4 g Total Fat (8.3 g Mono, 2.8 g Poly, 23.4 g Sat); 141 mg Cholesterol; 49 g Carbohydrate; 3 g Fibre; 14 g Protein; 427 mg Sodium

Pictured on page 11.

Safety tip: This recipe contains uncooked eggs. Make sure to use fresh, clean Grade A eggs. Keep frozen until consumed. Pregnant women, young children or the elderly are not advised to eat anything containing raw egg.

Banana Coconut Ice Cream Pie

Caramel ice cream topping	1/3 cup	75 mL
Graham cracker crust	1	1
Thinly sliced bananas (about 2 medium)	1 2/3 cups	400 mL
Vanilla ice cream, softened	2 3/4 cups	675 mL
Caramel ice cream topping	2/3 cup	150 mL
Medium unsweetened coconut, toasted (see Tip)	1/3 cup	75 mL

Sliced bananas, for garnish

Spread first amount of caramel ice cream topping over graham crust. Arrange banana slices over sauce.

Combine remaining 3 ingredients in medium bowl. Spread over bananas. Freeze. Let stand at room temperature for about 15 minutes before cutting.

Garnish with banana. Cuts into 8 wedges.

1 wedge: 379 Calories; 20.4 g Total Fat (0.1 g Mono, trace Poly, 10.5 g Sat); 83 mg Cholesterol; 45 g Carbohydrate; 11 g Fibre; 5 g Protein; 182 mg Sodium

Pictured on page 11.

Take a few minutes out of a busy morning to make this delightful treat, and it's ready to serve after dinner. Banana slices, chocolate curls, and drizzles of extra caramel sauce can make it even more impressive.

tip

When toasting nuts, seeds or coconut, cooking times will vary for each type of nut—so never toast them together. For small amounts, place ingredient in an ungreased shallow frying pan. Heat on medium for 3 to 5 minutes, stirring often, until golden. For larger amounts, spread ingredient evenly in an ungreased shallow pan. Bake in a 350°F (175°C) oven for 5 to 10 minutes, stirring or shaking often, until golden.

This pie can change every time you make it—devise delicious variations by trying different ice cream flavours.

variation

For something a little different, try making ice cream pie with gelato, which is Italian ice cream. The difference between gelato and traditional ice cream is that gelato contains less air, which gives it a dense, creamy texture and an intense flavour. Often it is made with milk rather than cream, making it lower in fat than its North American counterpart.

Arctic Freeze

VANILLA CRUST

Butter (or hard margarine)	1/3 cup	75 mL
Vanilla wafer crumbs (about 44 wafers)	1 1/4 cups	300 mL
Brown sugar, packed	2 tbsp.	30 mL

FILLING

Hot fudge ice cream topping	1 cup	250 mL
Vanilla ice cream, softened	4 cups	1 L
Apricot-flavoured liqueur (such as crème d'abricots) or peach schnapps (optional), see Note	1 tbsp.	15 mL
Frozen whipped topping, thawed	2 cups	500 mL

TOPPING

Butter (or hard margarine)	1 1/2 tsp.	7 mL
Sliced almonds	1/4 cup	60 mL
Granulated sugar	2 tsp.	10 mL
Ground cinnamon	1/4 tsp.	1 mL

Vanilla Crust: Melt butter in medium saucepan. Remove from heat. Add wafer crumbs and brown sugar. Stir well. Press firmly in bottom and up side of 9 inch (22 cm) pie plate. Bake in 350°F (175°C) oven for 10 minutes. Let stand on wire rack to cool.

Filling: Spread fudge ice cream topping over crust. Freeze until firm.

Spread ice cream over topping. Freeze until firm.

Stir liqueur into whipped topping in medium bowl. Spread over ice cream. Freeze.

Topping: Melt butter in medium saucepan on medium-low. Add remaining 3 ingredients. Heat and stir until almonds are toasted. Cool. Sprinkle over whipped topping. Freeze. Cuts into 8 wedges.

1 wedge: 618 Calories; 37.3 g Total Fat (5.5 g Mono, 1.3 g Poly, 22.4 g Sat); 149 mg Cholesterol; 63 g Carbohydrate; 2 g Fibre; 8 g Protein; 311 mg Sodium

Pictured at right.

Note: Choose a liqueur that complements your choice of ice cream. For example, coffee-flavoured liqueur (such as Kahlúa) with mocha ice cream, or mint-flavoured liqueur (such as crème de menthe) with mint chocolate chip ice cream.

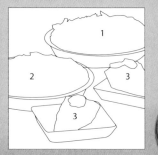

1. Artic Freeze, page 10
2. Banana Coconut Ice Cream Pie, page 9
3. Frozen Peanut Butter Pie, page 8

A chocolate ice cream pie with two succulent layers of juicy red raspberries. The preparation requires a little patience, but this pie tastes all the sweeter for the wait.

Chocolate Raspberry Pie

COOKIE CRUST

Butter (or hard margarine)	1/3 cup	75 mL
Vanilla wafer crumbs (about 44 wafers)	1 1/4 cups	300 mL

FILLING

Frozen raspberries in syrup, thawed	15 oz.	425 g
Cornstarch	1 tbsp.	15 mL
Chocolate ice cream, softened	3 cups	750 mL
Whipped cream (or envelope of dessert topping, prepared)	1 1/2 cups	375 mL
Chocolate ice cream topping	1 tbsp.	15 mL

Cookie Crust: Melt butter in medium saucepan. Remove from heat. Add wafer crumbs. Stir well. Press firmly in bottom and up side of 9 inch (22 cm) pie plate. Chill for 15 minutes.

Filling: Drain raspberry syrup into small saucepan. Reserve raspberries. Stir cornstarch into syrup. Heat and stir on medium for about 6 minutes until boiling and thickened. Remove from heat. Add reserved raspberries. Chill for 15 minutes.

Spread half of ice cream in crust. Spread half of raspberry mixture over ice cream. Freeze until firm. Repeat with remaining ice cream and raspberry mixture. Freeze until firm.

Top with whipped cream. Drizzle with chocolate ice cream topping. Freeze. Cuts into 8 wedges.

1 wedge: 577 Calories; 39.7 g Total Fat (7.6 g Mono, 1.4 g Poly, 23.9 g Sat); 174 mg Cholesterol; 51 g Carbohydrate; 3 g Fibre; 6 g Protein; 176 mg Sodium

Pictured at right.

A simple, light dessert to follow a heavy main course—the cold, crisp lemon flavour is the perfect sweet ending. Complete this luxurious lemon experience with a garnish of lemon zest and wedges. Can be frozen for up to eight weeks.

Frozen Lemon Cream Pie

Box of lemon-flavoured jelly powder (gelatin)	3 oz.	85 g
Granulated sugar	2 tbsp.	30 mL
Boiling water	1 cup	250 mL
Lemon juice	1/2 cup	125 mL
Grated lemon zest	2 tsp.	10 mL

(continued on next page)

Vanilla ice cream, softened	2 cups	500 mL
Graham cracker crust	1	1

Lemon zest, for garnish
Lemon slices, for garnish

Combine gelatin and sugar in medium bowl. Add water. Stir until gelatin and sugar are dissolved.

Add lemon juice and zest. Stir. Chill for about 1 1/2 hours, stirring and scraping down side of bowl occasionally, until syrupy. Do not let gelatin set too firmly or mixture will be lumpy when ice cream is added.

Add ice cream. Fold the gelatin mixture into the ice cream until smooth. Spread in crust. Freeze.

Garnish with zest and lemon slices. Cuts into 8 wedges.

1 wedge: 300 Calories; 14.9 g Total Fat (0 g Mono, 0 g Poly, 6.6 g Sat); 60 mg Cholesterol; 37 g Carbohydrate; trace Fibre; 4 g Protein; 178 mg Sodium

Pictured below.

1. Chocolate Raspberry Pie, page 12
2. Frozen Lemon Cream Pie, page 12

A flamboyant finale with a soft, marshmallow-textured meringue. A regular meringue may also be used. Pie can be frozen after adding Meringue Coating, and then baked at a later date.

You may wonder how you can bake ice cream and not have it melt into a puddle in your oven. The reason for this is the insulating power of meringue! In some recipes, sponge cake or pastry takes the place of meringue, but nothing quite matches its ability to protect the ice cream in this dessert from melting. Baked Alaska was originally known as omelette à la norvégienne, or Norwegian omelette, because of its cold appearance and icy centre. According to legend, it was renamed Baked Alaska in 1876 by New York's Delmonico's restaurant in honour of the U.S.'s acquisition of that state.

Baked Alaska Pie

CHOCOLATE GRAHAM CRUST		
Butter (or hard margarine)	1/3 cup	75 mL
Graham cracker crumbs	1 cup	250 mL
Granulated sugar	1/4 cup	60 mL
Cocoa, sifted if lumpy	3 tbsp.	50 mL
FILLING		
Strawberry ice cream, softened	4 cups	1 L
MERINGUE COATING		
Granulated sugar	1 cup	225 mL
Water	1/3 cup	75 mL
Vanilla extract	1 tsp.	5 mL
Cream of tartar	1/4 tsp.	1 mL
Egg whites (large)	2	2

Chocolate Graham Crust: Melt butter in medium saucepan. Remove from heat. Add next 3 ingredients. Stir until well mixed. Press firmly in bottom and up side of 9 inch (22 cm) pie plate. Chill for 15 minutes.

Filling: Spread ice cream in crust. Freeze.

Meringue Coating: Preheat oven to 500°F (260°C). Combine first 4 ingredients in small saucepan. Heat and stir on medium until mixture comes to a boil.

Beat egg whites in large bowl until foamy. Slowly add sugar mixture to egg whites, beating until combined. Beat for about 4 minutes until stiff peaks form. Spread over ice cream to edges of crust to seal. Bake for 3 to 4 minutes until browned. Serve immediately. Cuts into 8 wedges.

1 wedge: 496 Calories; 24.8 g Total Fat (2.4 g Mono, 0.7 g Poly, 15.0 g Sat); 115 mg Cholesterol; 64 g Carbohydrate; 1 g Fibre; 6 g Protein; 196 mg Sodium

Pictured on page 17.

Safety tip: The meringue in this recipe contains uncooked eggs. Make sure to use fresh, clean, Grade A eggs. Keep chilled and consume the same day it is prepared. Always discard leftovers. Pregnant women, young children or the elderly are not advised to eat anything containing raw egg.

Frosty Lime Pie

A refreshing dessert to keep in the freezer for summer barbecues.

CRUST		
Butter (or hard margarine)	1/3 cup	75 mL
Graham cracker crumbs	1 1/4 cups	275 mL
Granulated sugar	1/4 cup	60 mL
Cocoa, sifted if lumpy	3 tbsp.	50 mL
FILLING		
Egg yolk (large)	1	1
Cream cheese, softened	8 oz.	250 g
Granulated sugar	1/2 cup	125 mL
Lime juice	1/2 cup	125 mL
Grated lime zest	1 tsp.	5 mL
Egg white (large), room temperature	1	1
Whipping cream (or 1 envelope of dessert topping, prepared)	1 cup	250 mL
Drops of green liquid food colouring (optional)	2-4	2-4

Crust: Melt butter in medium saucepan. Remove from heat. Add next 3 ingredients. Stir until well mixed. Press firmly in bottom and up side of 9 inch (22 cm) pie plate. Bake in 350°F (180°C) oven for 10 minutes. Let stand on wire rack to cool.

Filling: Beat first 5 ingredients in medium bowl until smooth.

Beat egg white with clean beaters in small bowl until stiff peaks form. Fold into cream cheese mixture.

Beat cream, using same beaters and bowl until soft peaks form. Fold into cream cheese mixture. Fold in food colouring to tint a pale green if desired. Spread in crust. Freeze. Let stand at room temperature for about 15 minutes before cutting. Cuts into 8 wedges.

1 wedge: 412 Calories; 30.1 g Total Fat (5.9 g Mono, 1.3 g Poly, 18.7 g Sat); 115 mg Cholesterol; 33 g Carbohydrate; 1 g Fibre; 5 g Protein; 247 mg Sodium

Pictured on page 17.

Safety tip: This recipe contains uncooked eggs. Make sure to use fresh, clean Grade A eggs. Keep frozen until consumed. Pregnant women, young children or the elderly are not advised to eat anything containing raw egg.

A frosty delight on a gingersnap crust.

Frost On The Pumpkin

GINGERSNAP CRUST

Butter (or hard margarine)	1/3 cup	75 mL
Gingersnap crumbs (about 15 gingersnaps)	1 1/4 cups	275 mL
Granulated sugar	2 tbsp.	30 mL

FILLING

Canned pure pumpkin (no spices)	1 cup	250 mL
Brown sugar, packed	1/2 cup	125 mL
Ground cinnamon	1/2 tsp.	2 mL
Ground ginger	1/2 tsp.	2 mL
Ground nutmeg	1/4 tsp.	1 mL
Salt	1/4 tsp.	1 mL
Vanilla ice cream, softened	4 cups	1 L
Whipping cream (or 1 envelope of dessert topping, prepared)	1 cup	250 mL

Gingersnap Crust: Melt butter in medium saucepan. Remove from heat. Add gingersnap crumbs and sugar. Stir well. Press firmly in bottom and up side of 9 inch (22 cm) pie plate. Chill for 15 minutes.

Filling: Combine first 6 ingredients in large bowl. Add ice cream. Stir well.

Beat whipping cream in medium bowl until stiff peaks form. Fold into pumpkin mixture. Spread in crust. Freeze. Let stand at room temperature for 15 minutes before cutting. Cuts into 8 wedges.

1 wedge: 570 Calories; 38.0 g Total Fat (5.9 g Mono, 0.9 g Poly, 23.0 g Sat); 181 mg Cholesterol; 51 g Carbohydrate; 1 g Fibre; 7 g Protein; 301 mg Sodium

Pictured at right.

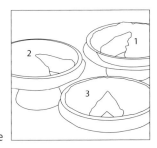

1. Baked Alaska Pie, page 14
2. Frosty Lime Pie, page 15
3. Frost On The Pumpkin, above

Everyone can tell at a glance that this delicate, yellow pie is homemade— a real scene stealer.

tip

Not sure how to get a baked pie shell? You can either purchase ready-made pie shells from the grocery store or make your own pastry. If you're using a store-bought pie crust, make sure to use a deep-dish, 9 inch crust instead of a regular-sized shell. Prick the bottom and sides all over with a fork before baking. If you make your own, cover the pastry with parchment paper up over the edge. Fill halfway with dried beans. Bake on the bottom rack in 375°F (190°C) oven for 15 minutes. Carefully remove paper and beans. You can save the beans for the next time you bake pastry. Bake for another 20 minutes until lightly browned. Be sure to let pastry cool before adding your filling.

Lemon Meringue Pie *A Classic!*

Water	2 cups	500 mL
Granulated sugar	3/4 cup	175 mL
Lemon juice	1/2 cup	125 mL
Butter (or hard margarine)	1 tbsp.	15 mL
Egg yolks (large)	3	3
Granulated sugar	1/2 cup	125 mL
Cornstarch	6 tbsp.	100 mL
Water	1/4 cup	50 mL
Salt	1/4 tsp.	1 mL
Baked 9 inch (22 cm) pie shell (see Tip)	1	1
Egg whites (large), room temperature	3	3
Cream of tartar	1/4 tsp.	1 mL
Granulated sugar	6 tbsp.	100 mL

Combine first 4 ingredients in medium saucepan. Bring to a boil on medium, stirring often until sugar is dissolved.

Whisk next 5 ingredients in small bowl. Slowly pour into boiling water mixture, stirring constantly, until boiling and thickened. Cook for about 2 minutes, stirring often. Remove from heat. Let stand for 30 minutes.

Spread lemon filling in pie shell.

Beat egg whites and cream of tartar in small bowl until soft peaks form. Add sugar, 1 tbsp. (15 mL) at a time, beating constantly until stiff peaks form and sugar is dissolved. Spoon egg white mixture over filling. Spread to edges of crust to seal. Bake in 350°F (175°C) oven for about 12 minutes until golden. Let stand at room temperature for at least 2 hours before serving. Cuts into 8 wedges.

1 wedge: 304 Calories; 8.3 g Total Fat (3.6 g Mono, 1.0 g Poly, 3.2 g Sat); 81 mg Cholesterol; 56 g Carbohydrate; trace Fibre; 3 g Protein; 209 mg Sodium

Pictured at right.

Safety tip: The meringue in this recipe contains uncooked eggs. Make sure to use fresh, clean, Grade A eggs. Keep chilled and consume the same day it is prepared. Always discard leftovers. Pregnant women, young children or the elderly are not advised to eat anything containing raw egg.

The sweetness of coconut fills every bite of this creamy, chilled pie.

Coconut Cream Pie *A Classic!*

Milk	2 1/4 cups	550 mL
Granulated sugar	2/3 cup	150 mL
All-purpose flour	1/2 cup	125 mL
Salt	1/4 tsp.	1 mL
Egg yolks (large)	3	3
Butter (or hard margarine)	2 tbsp.	30 mL
Vanilla extract	1 tsp.	5 mL
Shredded coconut	1 cup	250 mL
Baked 9 inch (22 cm) pie shell (see Tip, page 18)	1	1
Whipping cream (see Tip, page 22)	1 cup	250 mL
Granulated sugar	1 tbsp.	15 mL
Vanilla extract	3/4 tsp.	4 mL
Shredded coconut, toasted (see Tip, page 9)	1/3 cup	75 mL

Whisk first 4 ingredients in large saucepan. Boil on medium, stirring constantly until thickened.

Combine next 3 ingredients in small bowl. Slowly add about 1/2 cup (125 mL) hot milk mixture, stirring constantly. Slowly add egg yolk mixture to remaining hot milk mixture. Heat and stir constantly until boiling. Remove from heat.

Add first amount of coconut. Stir. Let stand for 15 minutes.

Spread coconut filling in pie shell. Cover with plastic wrap directly on surface to prevent skin from forming. Chill until firm.

Beat next 3 ingredients in medium bowl until soft peaks form. Spread over coconut mixture.

Sprinkle with second amount of coconut. Cuts into 8 wedges.

1 wedge: 436 Calories; 26.9 g Total Fat (7.6 g Mono, 1.5 g Poly, 16.2 g Sat); 129 mg Cholesterol; 44 g Carbohydrate; 1 g Fibre; 6 g Protein; 286 mg Sodium

Pictured at right.

Make for Thanksgiving or any time of year—always a favourite. Evaporated milk gives this pie the best texture. This recipe makes two pies, perfect for a large gathering.

tip

For a slightly different flavour, try combining the pumpkin filling with the spices and sugar in a saucepan and simmering them for five minutes on medium heat, stirring until thickened and glossy. Add the evaporated milk, return to a simmer briefly, remove from heat and let cool before pouring into pie shells.

tip

To save calories, substitute thawed frozen whipped topping for whipping cream, sugar and vanilla.

Pumpkin Pie *A Classic!*

Large eggs	4	4
Cans of pure pumpkin (no spices), 14 oz. (398 mL) each	2	2
Evaporated milk (or half-and-half cream)	3 cups	700 mL
Granulated sugar	1 1/4 cups	300 mL
Ground cinnamon	1 1/2 tsp.	7 mL
Ground ginger	1 tsp.	5 mL
Salt	1 tsp.	5 mL
Ground cloves	1/2 tsp.	2 mL
Ground nutmeg	1/2 tsp.	2 mL
Unbaked 9 inch (22 cm) pie shells	2	2
WHIPPED CREAM		
Whipping cream (see Tip)	2 cups	500 mL
Granulated sugar	2 tbsp.	30 mL
Vanilla extract	2 tsp.	10 mL

Whisk eggs in large bowl until frothy.

Add next 8 ingredients. Beat until smooth.

Pour into pie shells. Bake on bottom rack of 425°F (220°C) oven for 10 minutes. Reduce heat to 325°F (160°C). Bake 45 to 60 minutes until knife inserted near centre comes out clean. Let stand on wire racks until cool.

Whipped Cream: Beat all 3 ingredients in medium bowl until soft peaks form. Spread over pies before serving. Each pie cuts into 8 wedges, for a total of 16 wedges.

1 wedge: 387 Calories; 22.3 g Total Fat (3.8 g Mono, 0.6 g Poly, 12.6 g Sat); 115 mg Cholesterol; 40 g Carbohydrate; 2 g Fibre; 7 g Protein; 321 mg Sodium

Pictured at right.

Looks just like pumpkin pie—and almost tastes like it too! Serve with a dollop of whipped cream.

about sweet potatoes and yams

Many people confuse sweet potatoes with yams. While the two share some similarities, they come from different plants. Sweet potatoes are tubers of the morning glory plant native to Central America. Despite their name, they are not related to potatoes, and they are sweeter and less starchy than yams. The most commonly found variety in supermarkets has orange flesh and becomes soft and moist when cooked. Yams are tubers of a plant native to Africa and east Asia. They are starchier and earthier tasting than sweet potatoes; their flesh tends to be paler and has a drier, firmer texture when cooked.

buying and storing sweet potatoes

Choose firm sweet potatoes that don't have cracks, bruises, soft spots or any obvious signs of decay. Avoid buying refrigerated ones, and don't store raw sweet potatoes in the fridge as cold storage may change their flavour. Store in a dark, cool, ventilated place for about a week. Sweet potatoes can be frozen once cooked.

Sweet Potato Pie

Fresh unpeeled orange-fleshed sweet potatoes	1 1/2 lbs.	680 g
Salt	1/2 tsp.	2 mL
Water		
Evaporated milk (or half-and-half cream)	1 1/3 cups	300 mL
Granulated sugar	1/2 cup	125 mL
Brown sugar, packed	1/3 cup	75 mL
All-purpose flour	1 1/2 tbsp.	25 mL
Ground cinnamon	1/2 tsp.	2 mL
Ground nutmeg	1/4 tsp.	1 mL
Large eggs	2	2
Vanilla extract	1/4 tsp.	1 mL
Pastry for 9 inch (22 cm) deep dish pie shell		

Cook sweet potato in boiling salted water in large pot or Dutch oven on medium-high until tender. Drain. Rinse with cold water. Drain well. Peel and discard skin. Chop coarsely.

Process evaporated milk and sweet potato in blender or food processor until smooth.

Combine next 5 ingredients in large bowl.

Add eggs, vanilla and sweet potato mixture. Beat until smooth.

Roll out pastry on lightly floured surface to about 1/8 inch (3 mm) thickness. Line 9 inch pie plate. Trim, leaving 1/2 inch (12 mm) overhang. Roll under and crimp for a decorative edge. Spread potato mixture in pie shell. Bake on bottom rack in 425°F (220°C) oven for 15 minutes. Reduce heat to 350°F (175°C). Bake for about 45 minutes until knife inserted in centre comes out clean. Pie might puff up but will settle when cooling. Let stand on wire rack for at least 30 minutes before serving. Cuts into 8 wedges.

1 wedge: 313 Calories; 9.0 g Total Fat (0.6 g Mono, 0.1 g Poly, 4.4 g Sat); 73 mg Cholesterol; 50 g Carbohydrate; trace Fibre; 9 g Protein; 304 mg Sodium

Pictured at right.

A rich cream cheese layer is hidden beneath a sweet layer of chocolate.

chocolate whipped topping

Garnish your Double Decker Pie with this fluffy topping.

Semi-sweet chocolate chips	1 cup	250 mL
Envelopes of dessert topping (not prepared)	2	2
Milk	1 cup	250 mL
Vanilla	1 tsp.	5 mL

Melt chocolate chips in medium saucepan over hot water, or on low, stirring constantly, until smooth. Do not overheat. Cool to room temperature.

Beat topping mix, milk and vanilla in medium bowl until stiff. Add cooled chocolate. Beat to combine. Makes 5 cups (1.25 L).

1/4 cup (60 mL): 68 Calories; 1 g Protein; 4.5 g Total Fat; 7 g Carbohydrate; 13 mg Sodium; trace Fibre

Double Decker Pie

Butter (or hard margarine)	1/3 cup	75 mL
Chocolate wafer crumbs	1 1/2 cups	375 mL
Light cream cheese, softened	8 oz.	250 g
Icing (confectioner's) sugar	3/4 cup	175 mL
Milk	1/4 cup	60 mL
Vanilla extract	1 tsp.	5 mL
Envelope of unflavoured gelatin (about 1 tbsp., 15 mL)	1/4 oz.	7 g
Water	1/4 cup	60 mL
Semi-sweet chocolate baking squares (1 oz., 28 g, each), cut up	4	4
Envelope of dessert topping (not prepared), see Note	1	1
Milk	1/2 cup	125 mL

Heat butter in medium saucepan until melted. Remove from heat. Stir in wafer crumbs. Press firmly in bottom and up side of 9 inch (22 cm) pie plate. Bake in 350°F (175°C) oven for 10 minutes. Let stand on wire rack until cool.

Beat next 4 ingredients in medium bowl until smooth.

Sprinkle gelatin over water in small saucepan. Let stand for 1 minute. Heat and stir on low until gelatin is dissolved. Whisk into cream cheese mixture. Remove 1/2 cup (125 mL) of mixture to small bowl.

Heat chocolate in small saucepan on lowest heat, stirring often, until almost melted. Remove from heat. Stir until smooth. Add to mixture in small bowl. Stir well.

Beat dessert topping and second amount of milk in separate small bowl until stiff peaks form. Fold half of topping mixture into chocolate mixture. Fold remaining topping mixture into cream cheese mixture. Spread in crust. Spread chocolate mixture over top. Chill until set. Cuts into 8 wedges.

1 wedge: 348 Calories; 19.2 g Total Fat (3.1 g Mono, 1.2 g Poly, 11.4 g Sat); 35 mg Cholesterol; 38 g Carbohydrate; 1 g Fibre; 7 g Protein; 322 mg Sodium

Pictured at right.

Note: You can substitute 2 cups (500 mL) frozen whipped topping (thawed) for 1 envelope of dessert topping and milk.

This creamy custard pie should be well-chilled before serving.

Strawberry Custard Pie

Toasted sliced almonds (see Tip, page 9)	1/2 cup	125 mL
Baked 9 inch (22 cm) pie shell (see Tip, page 18), or graham cracker crust	1	1
Boxes of instant vanilla pudding powder, (4-serving size each)	2	2
Milk	2 cups	500 mL
Frozen whipped topping, thawed	1 cup	250 mL
Sliced fresh strawberries	1 1/2 cups	375 mL
STRAWBERRY GLAZE		
Mashed (or puréed) strawberries	1/2 cup	125 mL
Water	1/2 cup	125 mL
Granulated sugar	1/4 cup	60 mL
Cornstarch	1 tbsp.	15 mL

Scatter almonds in pie shell.

Beat pudding powder and milk in large bowl until smooth. Fold in whipped topping. Spread over almonds. Chill for 1 hour.

Spoon sliced strawberries over pudding mixture.

Strawberry Glaze: Combine all 4 ingredients in small saucepan. Bring to a boil on medium, stirring constantly, until thickened. Cool. Spoon over strawberries. Chill until set. Cuts into 8 wedges.

1 wedge: 254 Calories; 13.2 g Total Fat (2.4 g Mono, 0.9 g Poly, 5.6 g Sat); 9 mg Cholesterol; 30 g Carbohydrate; 2 g Fibre; 5 g Protein; 138 mg Sodium

Pictured at right.

A deliciously light-textured citrus pie that bursts with grapefruit flavour. Decorate with thin slices of pink grapefruit if you desire.

Grapefruit Chiffon Pie

Envelope of unflavoured gelatin (about 1 tbsp., 15 mL)	1/4 oz.	7 g
Grapefruit juice	1/4 cup	60 mL
Grapefruit juice	1 3/4 cups	400 mL
Granulated sugar	1/3 cup	75 mL
Grated grapefruit zest	1/2 tsp.	2 mL

(continued on next page)

Whipping cream (or 1 envelope of dessert topping, prepared)	1 cup	250 mL
Graham cracker crust	1	1

Grapefruit zest, for garnish

Sprinkle gelatin over first amount of grapefruit juice in small saucepan. Let stand for 1 minute. Heat and stir on low until gelatin is dissolved. Remove from heat.

Add next 3 ingredients. Stir until sugar is dissolved. Chill until mixture is starting to thicken and is syrupy.

Beat whipping cream in small bowl until stiff peaks form. Fold into grapefruit mixture. Spread in pie crust. Chill until set.

Garnish with grapefruit zest. Cuts into 8 wedges.

1 wedge: 277 Calories; 17.0 g Total Fat (3.2 g Mono, 0.4 g Poly, 8.0 g Sat); 41 mg Cholesterol; 29 g Carbohydrate; trace Fibre; 2 g Protein; 99 mg Sodium

Pictured below.

food fun

The word "chiffon," a term which started being used in relation to pies in the 1950s, perfectly describes the light, airy texture chiffon pies typically have. They usually consist of a custard filling lightened with beaten egg white or whipped cream, firmed up by the addition of gelatin. They're easy to make and great for entertaining.

Left: Strawberry Custard Pie, page 28
Right: Grapefruit Chiffon Pie, page 28

Classic cheesecake filling with a sweet sour cream topping. It's best made the day before, and leftovers may be frozen.

Cheesecake Pie

GRAHAM CRACKER CRUST

Butter (or hard margarine)	1/3 cup	75 mL
Graham cracker crumbs	1 1/4 cups	275 mL
Granulated sugar	2 tbsp.	30 mL

CHEESECAKE FILLING

Cream cheese, softened	12 oz.	375 g
Granulated sugar	1/2 cup	125 mL
Large eggs	2	2
Lemon juice	2 tbsp.	30 mL
Milk	2 tbsp.	30 mL
Grated lemon zest	1 tsp.	5 mL

SOUR CREAM TOPPING

Sour cream	1 1/2 cups	375 mL
Granulated sugar	2 tbsp.	30 mL

Graham Cracker Crust: Melt butter in small saucepan on low. Remove from heat. Add crumbs and sugar. Stir until well mixed. Press firmly in 9 inch (22 cm) pie plate.

Cheesecake Filling: Beat cream cheese and sugar in medium bowl until smooth. Add eggs, 1 at a time, beating well after each addition. Add next 3 ingredients. Stir. Spread in pie shell. Bake in 350°F (180°C) oven for about 25 minutes until firm.

Sour Cream Topping: Combine sour cream and sugar in small bowl. Spread over filling. Bake for 12 to 15 minutes until set. Let stand on wire rack until cool. Chill overnight. Cuts into 8 wedges.

1 wedge: 447 Calories; 31.7 g Total Fat (2.5 g Mono, 0.8 g Poly, 20.6 g Sat); 147 mg Cholesterol; 33 g Carbohydrate; trace Fibre; 7 g Protein; 308 mg Sodium

Pictured on page 3 and at right.

An unbaked pie that has a rich, chocolatey flavour, but a light, airy texture. Use a ready-made pie shell to save time.

about cocoa

A cocoa mix (sometimes called instant cocoa) is a blend of cocoa powder, dried milk powder and sugar. It's made to be combined with hot milk or hot water to produce a chocolatey beverage. Cocoa powder is made from roasted and crushed cocoa bean, is unsweetened and sold plain. When a recipe calls for cocoa powder, do not substitute cocoa mix.

Chocolate Chiffon Pie

Egg yolks (large)	4	4
Cocoa, sifted if lumpy	1/2 cup	125 mL
Granulated sugar	1/3 cup	75 mL
All-purpose flour	2 tbsp.	30 mL
Vanilla extract	1 tsp.	5 mL
Salt	1/4 tsp.	1 mL
Envelope of unflavoured gelatin (about 1 tbsp., 15 mL)	1/4 oz.	7 g
Water	1/2 cup	125 mL
Milk	1 cup	250 mL
Egg whites (large), room temperature	4	4
Cream of tartar	1/2 tsp.	2 mL
Granulated sugar	2/3 cup	150 mL
Baked 9 inch (22 cm) pie shell (see Tip, page 18)	1	1

Combine first 6 ingredients in small bowl.

Sprinkle gelatin over water in medium saucepan. Let stand for 1 minute. Add milk. Heat and stir on medium until gelatin is dissolved and mixture starts to boil. Add 2 tbsp. (30 mL) hot milk mixture to egg yolk mixture in small bowl. Stir. Slowly add egg yolk mixture back into hot milk mixture, stirring constantly until boiling and thickened. Chill for about 1 hour until starting to set. Mixture should be firm enough to spoon into soft mounds.

Beat egg whites and cream of tartar in medium bowl until soft peaks form. Add sugar, 1 tbsp. (15 mL) at a time, beating constantly until stiff peaks form and sugar is dissolved. Fold egg white mixture into gelatin mixture. Spread in pie shell. Chill for at least 4 hours until set. Cuts into 8 wedges.

1 wedge: 258 Calories; 8.2 g Total Fat (3.6 g Mono, 1.0 g Poly, 2.7 g Sat); 104 mg Cholesterol; 39 g Carbohydrate; 1 g Fibre; 7 g Protein; 224 mg Sodium

Pictured at right.

Safety tip: This recipe contains uncooked eggs. Make sure to use fresh, clean, Grade A eggs. Keep chilled and consume the same day it is prepared. Always discard leftovers. Pregnant women, young children or the elderly are not advised to eat anything containing raw egg.

A two-crust pie filled with a sour cream custard and fresh peaches.

tip

To peel peaches, immerse in boiling water for one minute. Transfer to cold water. Let stand for one minute. Remove from water. Remove peel.

buying peaches

If nothing's better than a good peach on a hot summer's day, nothing's worse than a bad one. Optimize your odds by choosing a peach with a well-defined cleft, a firm yet slightly yielding texture and no hint of green. Allow unripe peaches to ripen on your counter, or speed things up by placing them in a paper bag with an apple or banana—these fruits produce ethylene gas, which speeds up ripening. Finally, for maximum flavour, keep ripe peaches in your refrigerator for no more than a few days.

Sour Cream Peach Pie

Pastry for 2 crust 9 inch pie

Large egg, fork-beaten	1	1
Brown sugar, packed	1 cup	250 mL
Sour cream	1 cup	250 mL
All-purpose flour	1/3 cup	75 mL
Ground cinnamon	1/4 tsp.	1 mL
Sliced peeled, fresh peaches (about 3 medium peaches), see Tip	2 1/2 cups	575 mL
Granulated sugar	1/2 tsp.	2 mL

Divide pastry into 2 portions, making 1 portion slightly larger than the other. Shape each portion into slightly flattened disc. Roll out larger portion on lightly floured surface to about 1/8 inch (3 mm) thickness. Line 9 inch (22 cm) pie plate.

Combine next 5 ingredients in small bowl.

Place peach slices in pie shell. Spoon sour cream mixture over top. Spread over peaches. Roll out smaller portion of pastry on lightly floured surface to about 1/8 inch (3 mm) thickness. Dampen edge of pastry shell with water. Cover with remaining pastry. Trim and crimp decorative edge to seal.

Sprinkle with granulated sugar. Cut several small vents in top to allow steam to escape. Bake on bottom rack in 425°F (220°C) oven for 10 minutes. Reduce heat to 350°F (180°C) and bake about 40 minutes until golden brown and peaches are cooked (see Tip, page 42). Let stand on wire rack until cool. Cuts into 8 wedges.

1 wedge: 211 Calories; 5.7 g Total Fat (trace Mono, 0.1 g Poly, 3.7 g Sat); 47 mg Cholesterol; 37 g Carbohydrate; 1 g Fibre; 3 g Protein; 29 mg Sodium

Pictured on page 37.

Creamy Banana Pie

Brown sugar, packed	1/3 cup	75 mL
Cornstarch	3 tbsp.	50 mL
All-purpose flour	2 tbsp.	30 mL
Salt	1/4 tsp.	1 mL
Milk	2 cups	500 mL
Large eggs	2	2
Half-and-half cream	1/3 cup	75 mL
Butter (or hard margarine)	2 tsp.	10 mL
Vanilla extract	1 1/2 tsp.	7 mL
Medium bananas, diced	2	2
Baked 9 inch (22 cm) pie shell (see Tip, page 18), or graham cracker crust	1	1
Envelope of dessert topping (not prepared)	1	1
Milk	1/2 cup	125 mL
Vanilla extract	1/2 tsp.	2 mL

Sliced banana, for garnish

Combine first 4 ingredients in medium saucepan. Add first amount of milk. Heat and stir for about 6 minutes, stirring constantly, until boiling and thickened.

Whisk eggs and cream in small bowl. Slowly add egg mixture to hot milk mixture, stirring constantly for 1 to 2 minutes until boiling and thickened. Remove from heat.

Stir in next 3 ingredients.

Spread into pie shell. Cover with plastic wrap directly on surface to prevent skin from forming. Chill for at least 2 hours until set. Remove plastic wrap.

Beat next 3 ingredients in small bowl until stiff peaks form. Spread over filling.

Garnish with sliced banana just before serving. Cuts into 8 wedges.

1 wedge: 267 Calories; 11.4 g Total Fat (3.4 g Mono, 0.8 g Poly, 5.8 g Sat); 65 mg Cholesterol; 35 g Carbohydrate; 1 g Fibre; 6 g Protein; 253 mg Sodium

Pictured on page 37.

Banana cream pie made easy! This pie is light and fluffy with a smooth, creamy texture. A delicious finale to any meal.

A delicate shade of green with a delectable flavour—like biting into a cloud. Top with lime zest to complete the presentation and enhance the flavour.

about key limes

If you're using fresh lime juice for this recipe, don't worry about finding Key limes, which grow in the Florida Keys and are usually not easy to find outside major urban centres with well-stocked supermarkets or specialty food stores. Juice from commonly available limes works just as well.

Key Lime Pie

Envelope of unflavoured gelatin (about 1 tbsp., 15 mL)	1/4 oz.	7 g
Water	1/4 cup	50 mL
Egg yolks (large), fork-beaten	4	4
Granulated sugar	1/2 cup	125 mL
Lime juice	1/3 cup	75 mL
Grated lime zest	2 tsp.	10 mL
Salt	1/2 tsp.	2 mL
Drop of green liquid food colouring	1	1
Egg whites (large)	4	4
Granulated sugar	1/2 cup	125 mL
Whipping cream (or 1 envelope of dessert topping, prepared)	1 cup	250 mL
Baked 9 inch (22 cm) pie shell (see Tip, page 18)	1	1

Sprinkle gelatin over water in medium saucepan. Let stand for 1 minute. Heat and stir on low until gelatin is dissolved.

Combine next 6 ingredients in small bowl. Add to gelatin mixture. Beat well. Heat and stir on medium until boiling. Remove from heat. Let stand until cool. Chill, stirring occasional, until mixture is almost set.

Beat egg whites in medium bowl until soft peaks form. Add second amount of sugar, 1 tbsp. (15 mL) at a time, beating constantly until stiff peaks form and sugar is dissolved. Fold gelatin mixture into egg white mixture.

Beat cream in small bowl until stiff peaks form. Reserve 1/2 cup (125 mL) in small bowl for garnish. Fold remaining cream into egg white mixture. Spread in pie shell. Chill until set. Garnish with reserved whipped cream. Cuts into 8 wedges.

1 wedge: 321 Calories; 18.4 g Total Fat (6.6 g Mono, 1.4 g Poly, 9.3 g Sat); 143 mg Cholesterol; 35 g Carbohydrate; trace Fibre; 5 g Protein; 292 mg Sodium

Pictured at right.

Safety Tip: The meringue in this recipe contains uncooked eggs. Make sure to use fresh, clean Grade A eggs. Keep chilled and consume the same day it is prepared. Always discard leftovers. Pregnant women, young children or the elderly are not advised to eat anything containing raw egg.

1. Key Lime Pie, page 36
2. Sour Cream Peach Pie, page 34
3. Creamy Banana Pie, page 35

Enjoy a Prairie favourite. A delicate meringue covers a rich custard filling.

Flapper Pie

CRUST

Butter (or hard margarine)	1/4 cup	60 mL
Graham cracker crumbs	1 1/3 cups	325 mL
Brown sugar, packed	1/4 cup	60 mL

FILLING

Milk	2 cups	500 mL
Egg yolks (large)	3	3
Granulated sugar	1/4 cup	60 mL
Cornstarch	3 tbsp.	50 mL
Vanilla extract	1 tsp.	5 mL
Salt	1/4 tsp.	1 mL

MERINGUE

Egg whites (large), room temperature	3	3
Cream of tartar	1/4 tsp.	1 mL
Granulated sugar	3 tbsp.	50 mL

Crust: Melt butter in small saucepan on low. Remove from heat. Add crumbs and sugar. Stir until well mixed. Press firmly in 9 inch (22 cm) pie pan. Bake in 350°F (175°C) oven for 10 minutes. Let stand on wire rack until cool.

Filling: Heat milk in medium saucepan on medium until very hot and bubbles form around edge of saucepan.

Combine next 5 ingredients in small bowl. Slowly add egg mixture to hot milk mixture, stirring constantly for 1 to 2 minutes until boiling and thickened. Remove from heat. Cool for 30 minutes. Spread in crust.

Meringue: Beat egg whites and cream of tartar in small bowl until soft peaks form. Add sugar, 1 tbsp. (15 mL) at a time, beating constantly until stiff peaks form and sugar is dissolved. Spoon meringue over filling. Spread to edges of crust to seal. Bake in 350°F (175°C) oven for about 12 minutes until golden. Let stand on wire rack to cool. Chill until set. Cuts into 8 wedges.

1 wedge: 245 Calories; 9.4 g Total Fat (3.0 g Mono, 1.0 g Poly, 4.8 g Sat); 96 mg Cholesterol; 35 g Carbohydrate; trace Fibre; 6 g Protein; 257 mg Sodium

Pictured on page 41.

Safety Tip: The meringue in this recipe contains uncooked eggs. Make sure to use fresh, clean Grade A eggs. Keep chilled and consume the same day it is prepared. Always discard leftovers. Pregnant women, young children or the elderly are not advised to eat anything containing raw egg.

Nutty Mousse Pie

CHOCOLATE CRUST		
Butter (or hard margarine)	1/3 cup	75 mL
Chocolate wafer crumbs	1 1/4 cups	300 mL
FILLING		
Large marshmallows	30	30
Semi-sweet chocolate chips	1 cup	250 mL
Milk	1/2 cup	125 mL
Brown sugar, packed	1/3 cup	75 mL
Frozen whipped topping, thawed	2 cups	500 mL
TOPPING		
Frozen whipped topping, thawed	2 cups	500 mL
Chopped pecans	1/3 cup	75 mL

Chocolate Crust: Melt butter in small saucepan on low. Remove from heat. Add wafer crumbs. Stir until well mixed. Press firmly in 9 inch (22 cm) pie pan. Bake in 350°F (175°C) oven for 10 minutes. Let stand on wire rack to cool.

Filling: Combine first 4 ingredients in large saucepan. Heat on medium-low, stirring often, until melted and smooth. Chill for about 90 minutes, stirring and scraping down side of bowl often until ribbon of mixture stays on surface for about 30 seconds before becoming smooth. Mixture will resemble a thick paste.

Fold in whipped topping. Spread in pie shell.

Topping: Spread whipped topping over filling. Sprinkle with pecans. Chill overnight. Cuts into 8 wedges.

1 wedge: 439 Calories; 24.3 g Total Fat (7.1 g Mono, 2.3 g Poly, 13.8 g Sat); 21 mg Cholesterol; 58 g Carbohydrate; 2 g Fibre; 4 g Protein; 202 mg Sodium

A sweet chocolate crust holds this rich and creamy mousse filling. Must be prepared the day before.

about mousse

Mousse, French for "froth" or "foam," is a dish known for its richness and lightness. Mousses can be sweet or savoury; both kinds usually get their airy texture from the addition of beaten egg whites, but sweet mousses sometimes use whipping cream instead of egg whites. Gelatin is also often added for firmness. In this recipe, marshmallows take on the role of gelatin.

Pictured below

Luscious raspberries and silky almond custard rest on a tasty chocolate crust.

Chocolate Raspberry Flan

CHOCOLATE PASTRY

All-purpose flour	1 1/2 cups	375 mL
Granulated sugar	1/4 cup	60 mL
Cocoa, sifted if lumpy	2 tbsp.	30 mL
Cold butter (or hard margarine), cut up	1/2 cup	125 mL
Water	1/4 cup	60 mL

ALMOND CUSTARD

Egg yolks (large)	2	2
Homogenized milk	1 1/4 cups	300 mL
Granulated sugar	1/2 cup	125 mL
All-purpose flour	2 1/2 tbsp.	37 mL
Cornstarch	2 tbsp.	30 mL
Salt	1/8 tsp.	0.5 mL
Butter (or hard margarine)	2 tsp.	10 mL
Almond flavouring	1/2 tsp.	2 mL
Semi-sweet chocolate baking squares (1 oz., 28 g, each), chopped	2	2
Fresh raspberries	2 – 3 cups	500 – 750 mL

Chocolate Pastry: Combine first 3 ingredients in medium bowl. Cut in butter until mixture resembles coarse crumbs. Slowly add water, 1 tbsp. (15 mL) at a time, stirring with fork until mixture starts to come together. Do not overmix. Turn out pastry onto lightly floured surface. Shape into flattened disc. Wrap with plastic wrap. Chill for 30 minutes. Discard plastic wrap. Roll out pastry on lightly floured surface to fit greased 9 inch (22 cm) tart pan with fluted sides and removable bottom. Carefully lift pastry and press in bottom and up side of pan. Trim edge. Chill for 30 minutes. Place pan on ungreased baking sheet (see Tip). Cover pastry with parchment paper, extending paper over side of pan. Fill pan halfway with dried beans. Bake in 350°F (175°C) oven for about 25 minutes until crust on side is firm. Remove from oven. Carefully remove parchment paper and beans, reserving beans for next time you bake pastry. Bake for another 10 minutes until bottom is firm. Let stand on baking sheet on wire rack until cooled completely.

Almond Custard: Combine first 6 ingredients in small saucepan. Heat and stir on medium for about 7 minutes until boiling and thickened. Remove from heat.

Add butter and flavouring. Stir until butter is melted. Transfer to small heatproof bowl. Cover with plastic wrap directly on surface to prevent skin from forming. Cool to room temperature.

(continued on next page)

Heat chocolate in small heavy saucepan on lowest heat, stirring often, until almost melted. Remove from heat. Stir until smooth. Spread on bottom and side of crust. Let stand for about 15 minutes until set. Spread custard over chocolate. Arrange raspberries, open end down, in single layer on top of custard. Chill for at least 1 hour until custard is set. Cuts into 8 wedges.

1 wedge: *362 Calories; 16.8 g Total Fat (4.1 g Mono, 0.7 g Poly, 10.2 g sat); 89 mg Cholesterol; 50 g Carbohydrate; 1 g Fibre; 6 g Protein; 145 mg Sodium*

Pictured below.

Left: Chocolate Raspberry Flan, page 40
Right: Flapper Pie, page 38

Each portion is enough to make a 2 crust 9 inch (22 cm) pie, two single crust 9 inch (22 cm) pies or one pie with a lattice crust. Store in refrigerator for up to two weeks or in freezer for up to three months.

Favourite Pie Crust

All-purpose flour	5 cups	1.25 L
Brown sugar, packed	3 tbsp.	50 mL
Salt	2 tsp.	10 mL
Baking powder	1 tsp.	5 mL
Cold vegetable shortening (or lard), cut up	1 lb.	454 g
Large egg	1	1
Cold water, approximately	2/3 cup	150 mL
White vinegar	2 tbsp.	30 mL

Combine first 4 ingredients in large bowl. Cut in shortening until mixture resembles coarse crumbs.

Beat remaining 3 ingredients with fork in small bowl. Slowly add to flour mixture, stirring with fork, until mixture starts to come together. Do not overmix. Turn out onto work surface. Shape into 3 slightly flattened discs. Wrap each with plastic wrap. Chill for 1 hour before rolling. Makes 6 crusts.

1 crust: 1055 Calories; 76.4 g Total Fat (34.1 g Mono, 8.5 g Poly, 29.9 g Sat); 108 mg Cholesterol; 81 g Carbohydrate; 2 g Fibre; 11 g Protein; 880 mg Sodium

Pictured on front cover and at right.

As the saying goes, "apple pie without the cheese is like a kiss without a squeeze." If it's a sweeter treat you had in mind, serve with a scoop of ice cream and lay on ribbons of caramel sauce.

Apple Pie  A Classic!

Pastry for 2 crust 9 inch (22 cm) pie (Favourite Pie Crust, above)		
Granulated sugar	1 cup	250 mL
All-purpose flour	2 tbsp.	30 mL
Ground cinnamon	1/2 tsp.	2 mL
Chopped, or sliced, peeled cooking apples (such as McIntosh)	5 cups	1.25 L
Lemon juice	2 tsp.	10 mL
Granulated sugar	1/2 tsp.	2 mL

(continued on next page)

tip

If top crust browns too quickly, lay sheet of foil over top of pie and allow bottom crust to finish baking.

Divide pastry into 2 portions, making 1 portion slightly larger than the other. Shape each portion into slightly flattened disc. Roll out larger portion on lightly floured surface to about 1/8 inch (3 mm) thickness. Line 9 inch (22 cm) pie plate.

Combine next 3 ingredients in small bowl.

Stir apples and lemon juice in large bowl. Sprinkle with flour mixture. Stir well. Spread in pie shell. Roll out smaller portion of pastry on lightly floured surface to about 1/8 inch (3 mm) thickness. Dampen edge of pastry shell with water. Cover with remaining pastry. Trim and crimp decorative edge to seal.

Sprinkle with second amount of sugar. Cut several small vents in top to allow steam to escape. Bake on bottom rack in 350°F (175°C) oven for 45 to 55 minutes until golden and apples are tender (see Tip). Cuts into 8 wedges.

1 wedge: 385 Calories; 14.1 g Total Fat (trace Mono, trace Poly, 6.0 g Sat); 10 mg Cholesterol; 64 g Carbohydrate; 2 g Fibre; 2 g Protein; 201 mg Sodium

Pictured on front cover and below.

Apple Pie and Favourite Pie Crust, page 42

A golden crumb topping and a creamy white filling gives this apple pie our seal of approval. The tartness of the apple is a nice contrast to the sweet topping.

Forgotten Apple Pie

Large egg	1	1
All-purpose flour	2 tbsp.	30 mL
Salt	1/4 tsp.	1 mL
Sour cream	1 cup	250 mL
Granulated sugar	2/3 cup	150 mL
Vanilla extract	1/2 tsp.	2 mL
Chopped, or sliced, peeled cooking apples (such as McIntosh)	3 1/2 cups	875 mL
Unbaked 9 inch (22 cm) pie shell	1	1
All-purpose flour	1/3 cup	75 mL
Brown sugar, packed	1/3 cup	75 mL
Butter (or hard margarine), softened	1/4 cup	60 mL

Beat first 3 ingredients in medium bowl until smooth. Add next 3 ingredients. Beat until sugar is dissolved.

Add apple. Stir. Spread in pie shell. Bake on bottom rack in 400°F (205°C) oven for 10 minutes. Reduce heat to 350°F (175°C). Bake for 20 minutes.

Stir next 3 ingredients in small bowl until crumbly. Sprinkle over apple mixture. Bake for about 40 minutes until apples are tender. Cuts into 8 wedges.

1 wedge: 390 Calories; 18.3 g Total Fat (1.5 g Mono, 0.2 g Poly, 10.3 g Sat); 67 mg Cholesterol; 52 g Carbohydrate; 1 g Fibre; 4 g Protein; 235 mg Sodium

Pictured on page 45.

Another family favourite—saucy and delicious.

Raisin Pie

Raisins	2 cups	500 mL
Water	1 cup	250 mL
Brown sugar, packed	1 cup	250 mL
All-purpose flour	1/4 cup	60 mL
Salt	1/4 tsp.	1 mL
Lemon juice	2 tbsp.	30 mL
Grated lemon zest (optional)	1 tsp.	5 mL
Pastry for 2 crust 9 inch (22 cm) pie		
Granulated sugar	1/2 tsp.	2 mL

(continued on next page)

Bring raisins and water to a boil in small saucepan on medium. Cover. Reduce heat to medium-low. Simmer for 5 minutes.

Combine next 3 ingredients in small bowl. Add to raisins. Bring to a boil, stirring constantly, until thickened. Remove from heat.

Add lemon juice and zest. Stir. Cool for about 30 minutes.

Divide pastry into 2 portions, making 1 portion slightly larger than the other. Shape each portion into slightly flattened disc. Roll out larger portion on lightly floured surface to about 1/8 inch (3 mm) thickness. Line 9 inch (22 cm) pie plate. Spread raisin mixture in pie shell. Roll out smaller portion of pastry on lightly floured surface to about 1/8 inch (3 mm) thickness. Dampen edge of pastry shell with water. Cover with remaining pastry. Trim and crimp decorative edge to seal.

Sprinkle with granulated sugar. Cut several small vents in top to allow steam to escape. Bake on bottom rack in 400°F (205°C) oven for about 30 minutes until browned (see Tip, page 42). Cuts into 8 wedges.

1 wedge: 489 Calories; 14.0 g Total Fat (0 g Mono, 0 g Poly, 6.0 g Sat); 10 mg Cholesterol; 87 g Carbohydrate; 2 g Fibre; 3 g Protein; 293 mg Sodium

Pictured below.

food fun

Raisin pie dates back to at least the late 19th century. You will sometimes find it called funeral pie or rosina pie (rosina is German for "raisin"). The theory is that this pie was often traditionally served after funerals because it could be made ahead from commonly available ingredients and it stored well. Most recipes for raisin pie recommend using a double pie crust.

Left: Raisin Pie, page 44
Right: Forgotten Apple Pie, page 44

A wonderful blend of tart and sweet. Use your imagination to create cutouts to decorate the top.

about sanding sugar

Sanding sugar is a coarse decorating sugar that comes in white and various colours and is available at specialty kitchen stores.

Creating a decorative edge

Apple Cranberry Tart

Pastry for 2 crust 9 inch (22 cm) pie

Thinly sliced peeled tart apples (such as Granny Smith, about 5 large)	7 cups	1.75 L
Water	1/4 cup	60 mL
Granulated sugar	2/3 cup	150 mL
Dried cranberries	1/3 cup	75 mL
Grated lemon zest	1 tsp.	5 mL
Egg white (large), fork-beaten	1	1
Sanding (decorating) sugar (optional)	2 tbsp.	30 mL

Roll out 3/4 of pastry on lightly floured surface to fit ungreased 9 inch (22 cm) tart pan with fluted sides and removable bottom. Carefully lift pastry and press into bottom and up side of pan. Trim edge. Place pan on ungreased baking sheet (see Tip, page 40). Cover. Chill for 1 hour.

Combine apples and water in large saucepan. Bring to a boil. Cover. Reduce heat to medium. Simmer for about 8 minutes, stirring occasionally, until apple is tender.

Add next 3 ingredients. Stir. Remove from heat. Cool. Drain and discard liquid. Spread apple mixture in crust. Roll out remaining pastry on lightly floured surface to 1/8 inch (3 mm) thickness. Cut out shapes. Place around edge of tart.

Brush top with egg white. Sprinkle with sanding sugar. Bake on bottom rack in 375°F (190°C) oven for about 45 minutes until golden (see Tip, page 42). Cuts into 8 wedges.

1 wedge: 368 Calories; 14.1 g Total Fat (0 g Mono, trace Poly, 6.0 g Sat); 10 mg Cholesterol; 59 g Carbohydrate; 2 g Fibre; 3 g Protein; 207 mg Sodium

Pictured on page 47.

This pie has a pleasing blend of sweet and tart flovours, and can easliy be made ahead and frozen.

tip

To hasten the cooling process, stir mixture while resting pan in cold water in sink.

Raisin Rhubarb Pie

Raisins	2 cups	500 mL
Water	3/4 cup	175 mL
Brown sugar, packed	1 cup	250 mL
Granulated sugar	1/2 cup	125 mL
All-purpose flour	1/3 cup	75 mL
Salt	1/4 tsp.	1 mL
Lemon juice	1 tsp.	5 mL
Chopped fresh (or frozen, thawed) rhubarb	1 1/2 cups	375 mL
Pastry for 2 crust 9 inch (22 cm) pie		
Granulated sugar	1/2 tsp.	2 mL

Bring raisins and water to a boil in medium saucepan. Cover. Reduce heat to medium-low. Simmer for 5 minutes.

Combine next 4 ingredients in small bowl. Stir into raisins until mixture is boiling and thickened. Remove from heat.

Add lemon juice and rhubarb. Stir well. Let stand until cool (see Tip).

Divide pastry into 2 portions, making 1 portion slightly larger than the other. Shape each portion into slightly flattened disc. Roll out larger portion on lightly floured surface to about 1/8 inch (3 mm) thickness. Line 9 inch (22 cm) pie plate. Spread rhubarb mixture in pie shell. Roll out smaller portion of pastry on lightly floured surface to about 1/8 inch (3 mm) thickness. Dampen edge of pastry shell with water. Cover with remaining pastry. Trim and crimp decorative edge to seal.

Sprinkle with second amount of sugar. Cut several small vents in top to allow steam to escape. Bake on bottom rack in 375°F (190°C) oven for about 40 minutes until golden (see Tip, page 42) and rhubarb is tender. Cuts into 8 wedges.

1 wedge: 545 Calories; 14.1 g Total Fat (trace Mono, trace Poly, 6.0 g Sat); 10 mg Cholesterol; 101 g Carbohydrate; 3 g Fibre; 4 g Protein; 294 mg Sodium

Pictured on page 51.

Date Pie

Chopped pitted dates	2 cups	500 mL
Water	1 cup	250 mL
Granulated sugar	1/4 cup	60 mL
Milk	1 cup	225 mL
Cornstarch	2 tbsp.	30 mL
Egg yolks (large)	3	3
Vanilla extract	1 tsp.	5 mL
Baked 9 inch (22 cm) deep dish pie shell (see Tip, page 18)	1	1
MERINGUE		
Egg whites (large)	3	3
Cream of tartar	1/4 tsp.	1 mL
Granulated sugar	6 tbsp.	100 mL

Meringue swirls are a great complement to the sweet date flavour.

tip

Cut meringue pies with hot, wet knife.

Combine first 3 ingredients in small saucepan on medium. Bring to a boil. Cover. Reduce heat to medium-low. Simmer for about 5 minutes until dates are soft and water is absorbed.

Stir milk into cornstarch in small cup. Stir into date mixture. Bring to a boil, stirring constantly, until boiling and thickened.

Combine egg yolks and vanilla in small bowl. Add 2 tbsp. (30 mL) hot mixture. Stir. Slowly add egg yolk mixture to date mixture, stirring constantly until boiling and thickened. Spread in pie shell. Cool slightly.

Meringue: Beat egg whites and cream of tartar in medium bowl until soft peaks form. Add sugar, 1 tbsp. (15 mL) at a time, beating constantly until stiff peaks form and sugar is dissolved. Spoon egg white mixture over filling. Spread to edges of crust to seal. Bake in 375°F (190°C) oven for about 10 minutes until golden. Let stand on wire rack to cool to room temperature. Chill for at least 8 hours or overnight. Cuts into 8 wedges.

1 wedge: 380 Calories; 12.0 g Total Fat (0.8 g Mono, 0.3 g Poly, 2.8 g Sat); 79 mg Cholesterol; 66 g Carbohydrate; 3 g Fibre; 5 g Protein; 180 mg Sodium

Pictured on page 51.

Safety Tip: The meringue in this recipe contains uncooked eggs. Make sure to use fresh, clean Grade A eggs. Keep chilled and consume the same day it is prepared. Always discard leftovers. Pregnant women, young children or the elderly are not advised to eat anything containing raw egg.

You can still bake pies on a hot day—use the barbecue and you won't heat up the house. This sweet pie has a rich, burgundy filling that holds its shape well and cuts easily.

about pie thickeners

If you want to thicken the filling of a pie, don't feel you must limit yourself to flour. Cornstarch, arrowroot, potato starch and tapioca all have three times the thickening power of flour, and each is appropriate for a different kind of pie. A stiff thickener like cornstarch works well in a pie with fruit such as cherries, which release a lot of juice but do not get very soft during the baking process. Tapioca is a better thickener in pies with fruit that breaks down and mixes with its own juices, such as raspberries or peaches.

Apple Raspberry Pie

Pastry for 2 crust 9 inch (22 cm) pie

Granulated sugar	3/4 cup	175 mL
Minute tapioca	3 tbsp.	50 mL
Ground cinnamon	1/4 tsp.	1 mL
Sliced peeled cooking apple (such as McIntosh)	2 2/3 cups	650 mL
Fresh (or frozen, thawed) raspberries	1 1/2 cups	375 mL
Granulated sugar	1/4 tsp.	1 mL

Divide pastry into 2 portions, making 1 portion slightly larger than the other. Shape each portion into slightly flattened disc. Roll out larger portion on lightly floured surface to about 1/8 inch (3 mm) thickness. Line 9 inch (22 cm) pie plate.

Combine next 3 ingredients in large bowl. Add apple and raspberries. Stir well. Spread in pie shell. Roll out smaller portion on lightly floured surface to about 1/8 inch (3 cm) thickness. Dampen edge of pastry shell with water. Cover with remaining pastry. Trim and crimp decorative edge to seal.

Sprinkle with second amount of sugar. Cut several small vents in top to allow steam to escape. Place on ungreased baking sheet. Preheat gas barbecue to high. Place baking sheet on grill. Turn burner under pie to low and leave opposite burner on high. Cook for about 70 minutes, rotating pie at halftime, until apple is tender and crust is golden (see Tip, page 42). Cuts into 8 wedges.

1 wedge: 355 Calories; 14.1 g Total Fat (0 g Mono, trace Poly, 6.0 g Sat); 10 mg Cholesterol; 57 g Carbohydrate; trace Fibre; 2 g Protein; 200 mg Sodium

Pictured at right.

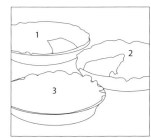

1. Raisin Rhubarb Pie, page 48
2. Date Pie, page 49
3. Apple Raspberry Pie, above

Fresh peach flavour is a little bit of summer to savour.

Blind baking is a great way to pre-bake your crusts and prevent them from rising unevenly.

Peach Pie

Granulated sugar	1 cup	250 mL
Water	1 cup	250 mL
Cornstarch	1/4 cup	60 mL
Corn syrup	2 tbsp.	30 mL
Lemon juice	1 tsp.	5 mL
Box of peach-flavoured jelly powder (gelatin)	3 oz.	85 g
Chopped peeled fresh peaches (about 4), see Tip, page 34	3 cups	750 mL
Baked 9 inch (22 cm) pie shell (see Tip, page 18)	1	1
Frozen whipped topping (thawed), for garnish	2 cups	500 mL
Peach slices, for garnish (optional)		

Combine first 5 ingredients in large saucepan. Bring to a boil, stirring constantly. Reduce heat to medium. Simmer for 3 minutes. Remove from heat.

Add jelly powder. Stir until dissolved. Cool slightly (see Tip, page 48).

Add peaches. Stir. Spread in pie shell. Chill for at least 3 hours until set.

Garnish with whipped topping and peach slices. Cuts into 8 wedges.

1 wedge: 271 Calories; 5.3 g Total Fat (2.5 g Mono, 0.7 g Poly, 1.7 g Sat); 0 mg Cholesterol; 56 g Carbohydrate; 1 g Fibre; 2 g Protein; 149 mg Sodium

Pictured at right.

Mince Pie

Brown sugar, packed	1/2 cup	125 mL
All-purpose flour	1/4 cup	60 mL
Ground cinnamon	1/2 tsp.	2 mL
Ground cloves	1/4 tsp.	1 mL
Ground nutmeg	1/4 tsp.	1 mL
Salt	1/4 tsp.	1 mL
Chopped peeled cooking apple	1 cup	250 mL
Grated peeled potato	1 cup	250 mL
Water	1/2 cup	125 mL
White vinegar	2 tbsp.	30 mL

(continued on next page)

| Frozen 9 inch (22 cm) pie shells, thawed according to package directions | 2 | 2 |
| Granulated sugar | 1/2 tsp. | 2 mL |

Whipped cream, for garnish
Apple slices, for garnish

Combine first 6 ingredients in large bowl.

Add next 4 ingredients. Stir well.

Brush edge of 1 pie shell with water. Spread apple mixture in shell. Roll out remaining pie shell to fit over top. Trim and crimp decorative edge to seal.

Sprinkle with granulated sugar. Cut several small vents in top to allow steam to escape. Bake on bottom rack in 350°F (175°C) oven for about 60 minutes until browned (see Tip, page 42).

Garnish with whipped cream and apple. Cuts into 8 wedges.

1 wedge: 330 Calories; 15.3 g Total Fat (0.5 g Mono, 0.2 g Poly, 6.5 g Sat); 10 mg Cholesterol; 48 g Carbohydrate; 1 g Fibre; 3 g Protein; 285 mg Sodium

Pictured below.

A warm pie with warm flavours—try serving it à la mode, too. Use frozen pie shells for ease and convenience.

Left: Mince Pie, page 52
Right: Peach Pie, page 52

Everyone will save room for a slice of this lovely, fresh raspberry pie. Make it a day or two ahead of your picnic and store well-wrapped in the refrigerator—allow it to lose its chill before serving for maximum flavour.

tip

If you don't have a food processor, combine flour and icing sugar in medium bowl. Cut in butter until crumbly. Stir in egg yolks and water with fork.

about pie crusts

Butter makes a richer tasting crust than lard or shortening, but some people find a buttery dough hard to work with. Lard or shortening make a dough that most find easy to work with and crusts that are very flaky, but relatively tasteless. Some pie crust recipes solve this dilemma by including both butter and shortening, thereby creating a dough that is easy to handle and richly flavoured.

Deluxe Raspberry Pie

BUTTER PASTRY

All-purpose flour	2 cups	500 mL
Cold butter (or hard margarine), cut up	3/4 cup	175 mL
Icing (confectioner's) sugar	1/2 cup	125 mL
Egg yolks (large)	2	2
Cold water	1/4 cup	60 mL

RASPBERRY FILLING

Fresh raspberries	6 cups	1.5 L
Lemon juice	1 tbsp.	15 mL
Grated lemon zest	1 tsp.	5 mL
Granulated sugar	2/3 cup	150 mL
Cornstarch	1/4 cup	60 mL
Ground cinnamon	3/4 tsp.	4 mL
Egg yolk (large), fork-beaten	1	1
Granulated sugar	2 tsp.	10 mL

Fresh raspberries, for garnish
Whipped cream, for garnish
Sprigs of fresh mint, for garnish

Butter Pastry: Process first 3 ingredients in food processor until mixture is crumbly (see Tip).

Add egg yolks and water. Pulse with on/off motion until mixture starts to come together. Do not over process. Turn out pastry onto work surface. Divide into 2 equal portions. Wrap with plastic wrap. Chill for 30 minutes. Roll out 1 portion on lightly floured surface to 1/8 inch (3 mm) thickness. Line 9 inch (22 cm) pie plate. Cover with plastic wrap. Chill for 15 minutes.

Raspberry Filling: Combine first 3 ingredients in medium bowl.

Stir next 3 ingredients in small bowl. Sprinkle over raspberry mixture. Stir well. Spread in pie shell. Roll out remaining pastry on lightly floured surface to 1/8 inch (3 mm) thickness. Dampen edge of pastry shell with water. Cover with remaining pastry. Trim and crimp decorative edge to seal. Cover. Chill for 15 minutes.

Brush pastry with egg yolk. Sprinkle with granulated sugar. Cut several small vents in top to allow steam to escape. Bake on bottom rack in 375°F (190°C) oven for about 1 hour until pastry is golden. Let stand on wire rack to cool.

(continued on next page)

Garnish with raspberries, whipped cream and mint. Cuts into 8 wedges.

1 wedge: 422 Calories; 18.7 g Total Fat (5.2 g Mono, 0.9 g Poly, 11.4 g Sat); 122 mg Cholesterol; 64 g Carbohydrate; 1 g Fibre; 5 g Protein; 124 mg Sodium

Pictured below.

Note: When cooking with a frozen baking dish, make sure the dish is designed to withstand the sudden temperature change from freezer to oven.

Tart rhubarb topped with sweetness—like a rhubarb crisp in a crust. Delicious served with ice cream.

food fun

Streusel is a German word meaning "sprinkle" or "strew."

about rhubarb

Hothouse rhubarb is sweeter and more tender than field-grown rhubarb, which tends to be more tart and has stalks that benefit from peeling. Cut off any and all leaves from the stalks. Never eat the rhubarb leaves; they contain a poisonous compound called oxalic acid.

For a delicious change of pace, try this crust-on-the-top version of pie. During the short plum season, this becomes an extra special treat.

Pinched Edge

Strawberry Rhubarb Streusel Pie

Chopped fresh (or frozen, thawed) rhubarb	3 cups	750 mL
Sliced fresh (or frozen, thawed) strawberries	1 cup	250 mL
Granulated sugar	1 cup	250 mL
All-purpose flour	3 tbsp.	50 mL
Lemon juice	1/2 tsp.	2 mL
Unbaked 9 inch (22 cm) pie shell	1	1

TOPPING		
All-purpose flour	2/3 cup	150 mL
Brown sugar, packed	1/2 cup	125 mL
Ground cinnamon	1/2 tsp.	2 mL
Cold butter (or hard margarine)	1/3 cup	75 mL

Combine first 5 ingredients in large bowl. Spread in pie shell.

Topping: Combine first 3 ingredients in large bowl. Cut in butter until crumbly. Sprinkle over rhubarb mixture. Bake on bottom rack in 375°F (190°C) oven for about 50 minutes until golden. Cuts into 8 wedges.

1 wedge: 395 Calories; 14.7 g Total Fat (2.0 g Mono, 0.4 g Poly, 7.8 g Sat); 25 mg Cholesterol; 65 g Carbohydrate; 1 g Fibre; 3 g Protein; 161 mg Sodium

Pictured at right.

Deep Plum Pie

Prune plums, halved and pitted (about 20 large)	3 lbs.	1.4 kg
Granulated sugar	1 1/2 cups	375 mL
Minute tapioca	1/3 cup	75 mL

PASTRY		
All-purpose flour	1 1/2 cups	375 mL
Salt	1/4 tsp.	1 mL
Cold butter (or hard margarine), cut up	1/2 cup	125 mL
Ice water	4 1/2 tbsp.	67 mL
Granulated sugar	2 tsp.	10 mL

(continued on next page)

Combine first 3 ingredients in large bowl. Spread in greased 9 x 13 inch (22 x 33 cm) baking dish.

Pastry: Combine flour and salt in separate large bowl. Cut in butter until mixture resembles coarse crumbs. Slowly add water, stirring with fork until mixture starts to come together. Do not overmix. Shape into slightly flattened disc. Wrap with plastic wrap. Chill for 1 hour. Roll out between 2 sheets of waxed paper to 10 x 14 inch (25 x 35 cm) rectangle. Discard top sheet of waxed paper. Invert pastry over plums. Discard waxed paper. Crimp decorative edge.

Sprinkle with second amount of sugar. Cut several small vents in top to allow steam to escape. Bake in 350°F (175°C) oven for about 1 hour until plums are soft and bubbling and crust is golden. Serves 12 to 15.

1 serving: 285 Calories; 7.8 g Total Fat (2.1 g Mono, 0.3 g Poly, 4.8 g Sat); 20 mg Cholesterol; 54 g Carbohydrate; 2 g Fibre; 2 g Protein; 102 mg Sodium

Pictured below.

Left: Deep Plum Pie, page 56
Right: Strawberry Rhubarb Streusel Pie, page 56

Fluted Edge

Forked Edge

Sweet ginger and banana-flavoured pie with a nutty streusel top. Perfect with ice cream.

food fun

Macadamia trees grow wild in their native Australia, but they're also cultivated as a food crop there as well as in Hawaii, California, Central and South America, Israel and South Africa. The tree was named for Australian chemist and natural historian John MacAdam, a colleague of the botanist who first described the genus. Macadamia nuts are extremely rich tasting because they have a very high oil content, and they should be stored in the refrigerator or freezer to prevent them from going rancid.

Banana Streusel Pie

Sliced bananas (about 5 medium)	4 cups	1 L
Pineapple juice	3/4 cup	175 mL
Brown sugar, packed	1/3 cup	75 mL
Cornstarch	2 tsp.	10 mL
Grated lime zest	1 tsp.	5 mL
Ground ginger	1/2 tsp.	2 mL
Ground cardamom	1/8 tsp.	0.5 mL
Pastry for 9 inch (22 cm) pie shell		
MACADAMIA STREUSEL TOPPING		
All-purpose flour	1/2 cup	125 mL
Brown sugar, packed	1/2 cup	125 mL
Cold butter (or hard margarine), cut up	1/4 cup	60 mL
Coarsely chopped macadamia nuts	1/3 cup	75 mL

Combine banana and pineapple juice in medium bowl. Toss until well coated. Drain juice into small saucepan.

Add brown sugar and cornstarch to juice. Heat and stir on medium for 7 to 8 minutes until boiling and thickened. Let stand for 5 minutes.

Add next 3 ingredients and thickened juice mixture to banana mixture. Stir.

Roll out pastry on lightly floured surface to about 1/8 inch (3 mm) thickness. Line 9 inch (22 cm) pie plate. Trim, leaving 1/2 inch (12 mm) overhang. Roll under and crimp decorative edge. Spread banana mixture in pie shell.

Macadamia Streusel Topping: Combine flour and brown sugar in separate medium bowl. Cut in butter until mixture resembles coarse crumbs.

Add macadamia nuts. Stir. Sprinkle over banana filling. Bake on bottom rack in 375°F (190°C) oven for about 35 to 40 minutes until top is golden and filling is bubbling. Cuts into 8 wedges.

1 wedge: 404 Calories; 17.2 g Total Fat (4.8 g Mono, 0.4 g Poly, 7.4 g Sat); 20.1 mg Cholesterol; 62 g Carbohydrate; 3 g Fibre; 3 g Protein; 151 mg Sodium

Pictured on page 61.

Pear Tart With Maple Sauce

Pastry for 9 inch (22 cm) pie shell

Butter (or hard margarine), softened	1/4 cup	60 mL
Granulated sugar	1/3 cup	75 mL
Large egg	1	1
Almond extract	1/2 tsp.	2 mL
Ground almonds	2/3 cup	150 mL
All-purpose flour	3 tbsp.	50 mL
Seedless raspberry jam (not jelly)	1/4 cup	60 mL
Can of pear halves in light syrup, drained, blotted dry, cut into thin wedges	28 oz.	796 mL
Brown sugar, packed	3 tbsp.	50 mL
MAPLE SAUCE		
Maple (or maple-flavoured) syrup	1/2 cup	125 mL
Butter (or hard margarine)	1/3 cup	75 mL
Whipping cream	1/3 cup	75 mL

Roll out pastry on lightly floured surface to fit ungreased 9 inch (22 cm) tart pan with fluted sides and removable bottom. Carefully lift pastry and press into bottom and up side of pan. Trim edge. Place pan on ungreased baking sheet (see Tip, page 40).

Beat butter and granulated sugar in medium bowl. Add egg and extract. Beat well. Add almonds and flour. Stir until mixture resembles fine paste.

Spread jam on bottom of crust. Spread almond mixture over jam. Arrange pear wedges, slightly overlapping, in fan pattern on top of almond mixture to cover.

Sprinkle with brown sugar. Bake on bottom rack in 375°F (190°C) oven for about 1 1/4 hours until pastry is golden and pear just starts to turn golden brown. Let stand in pan on wire rack to cool.

Maple Sauce: Combine all 3 ingredients in small saucepan on medium. Heat and stir until butter is melted and mixture is boiling. Boil gently for about 3 minutes, stirring occasionally, until thickened. Brush 1/4 cup (60 mL) on top of tart. Spoon remaining sauce over individual servings. Cuts into 8 wedges.

1 wedge: 538 Calories; 28.7 g Total Fat (7.1 g Mono, 1.7 g Poly, 14.2 g Sat); 81 mg Cholesterol; 69 g Carbohydrate; 4 g Fibre; 4 g Protein; 215 mg Sodium

Pictured on page 61.

This delicious dessert is sure to impress! Pears are an excellent complement to sweet maple syrup.

variation

Omit the Maple Sauce. Heat 1/4 cup (60 mL) of seedless raspberry jam in a small microwave-safe bowl on medium (50%) until melted. Brush on top of the tart before cutting it into wedges

make ahead

The baked tart may be covered and stored in the refrigerator for up to 24 hours. Bring to room temperature before serving. The sauce may be stored in an airtight container in the refrigerator for up to 24 hours. Reheat it in a medium saucepan on low heat before brushing over the tart.

A perfect recipe for the rookie cook—it's very easy, yet looks like a pastry chef baked it. The sweet, juicy peaches work wonderfully with the slightly tart blueberries.

Rustic Peach And Blueberry Pie

COOKING OIL PASTRY

All-purpose flour	2 cups	500 mL
Baking powder	1 tbsp.	15 mL
Salt	1/2 tsp.	2 mL
Cold water	1/2 cup	125 mL
Cooking oil	1/2 cup	125 mL

FILLING

Brown sugar, packed	1/3 cup	75 mL
All-purpose flour	2 tbsp.	30 mL
Ground cinnamon	1/4 tsp.	1 mL
Canned sliced peaches, drained	4 cups	1 L
Fresh (or frozen, thawed) blueberries	2 cups	500 mL
Icing (confectioner's) sugar	1 tbsp.	15 mL

Cooking Oil Pastry: Combine first 3 ingredients in large bowl.

Add water and cooking oil, stirring with fork until mixture starts to come together. Do not overmix. Turn out pastry onto lightly floured surface. Shape into large circle. Roll out to about 16 inches (40 cm) in diameter. Transfer to ungreased 12 inch (30 cm) pizza pan, allowing pastry to hang over sides.

Filling: Combine first 3 ingredients in large bowl. Add peaches and blueberries. Stir. Spoon peach mixture onto centre of pastry, leaving 4-inch (10 cm) border. Fold a section of edge up and over edge of filling. Repeat with next section, allowing pastry to overlap so that folds are created. Repeat until pastry border is completely folded around filling. Bake on bottom rack in 375°F (190°C) oven for about 45 minutes until crust is golden and fruit is tender. Let stand in pan on wire rack to cool.

Dust fruit and pastry with icing sugar. Serves 12.

1 serving: 250 Calories; 9.5 g Total Fat (5.4 g Mono, 2.7 g Poly, 0.7 g Sat); 0 mg Cholesterol; 41 g Carbohydrate; 3 g Fibre; 3 g Protein; 241 mg Sodium

Pictured at right.

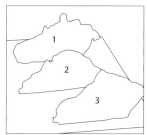

1. Banana Streusel Pie, page 58
2. Rustic Peach And Blueberry Pie, above
3. Pear Tart With Maple Sauce, page 59

Try this with either the pastry or the crumb topping—both are sure to be a hit.

crumb topping

If you use this topping, you will need only one 9 inch pie crust. Use pastry to line bottom of pie plate.

All-purpose flour	2/3 cup	150 mL
Brown sugar, packed	6 tbsp.	100 mL
Butter (or hard margarine)	6 tbsp.	100 mL
Ground cinnamon	1/2 tsp.	2 m
Salt	1/4 tsp.	1 mL

Crumb Topping: Stir all 5 ingredients in medium bowl until crumbly. Sprinkle over fruit. Bake on bottom rack in 400°F (205°C) oven for 15 minutes. Reduce heat to 350°F (175°C). Bake for about 35 minutes until golden. Let stand on wire rack to cool. Cuts into 8 wedges.

1 wedge: 148 Calories; 8.5 g Total Fat (2.2 g Mono, 0.3 g Poly, 5.4 g Sat); 23 mg Cholesterol; 18 g Carbohydrate; trace Fibre; 1 g Protein; 137 mg Sodium

An absolute must! This fruity pie has a real burst of flavour, and uses deliciously chewy meringue as a base instead of a pastry crust.

Cranberry Pear Pie

Cans of pear halves in juice (14 oz., 398 mL each) drained and sliced (see Note)	4	4
Fresh (or frozen) cranberries, halved	1 cup	250 mL
Granulated sugar	3/4 cup	175 mL
All-purpose flour	3 tbsp.	50 mL
Pastry for 2 crust 9 inch (22 cm) pie shell		
Granulated sugar	1/2 tsp.	2 mL

Combine first 4 ingredients in large bowl.

Divide pastry into 2 portions, making 1 portion slightly larger than the other. Shape each portion into slightly flattened disc. Roll out larger portion on lightly floured surface to about 1/8 inch (3 mm) thickness. Line 9 inch (22 cm) pie plate.

Spread fruit mixture in shell. Roll out smaller portion of pastry on lightly floured surface to about 1/8 inch (3 mm) thickness. Dampen edge of pastry shell with water. Cover with remaining pastry. Trim and crimp decorative edge to seal. Bake on bottom rack in 400°F (205°C) oven for 15 minutes. Reduce heat to 350°F (175°C). Bake for about 35 minutes until golden brown (see Tip, page 42). Let stand on wire rack to cool. Cuts into 8 wedges.

1 wedge: 477 Calories; 14.4 g Total Fat (0.1 g Mono, 0.1 g Poly, 6.0 g Sat); 10 mg Cholesterol; 87 g Carbohydrate; 6 g Fibre; 3 g Protein; 210 mg Sodium

Pictured at right.

Note: If using fresh pears, peel and slice about 5 pears to make 4 cups (1 L). Use 1/3 cup (75 mL) flour instead of 3 tbsp. (50 mL).

Berry Angel Pie

Egg whites (large), room temperature	3	3
Granulated sugar	1 cup	225 mL
Vanilla extract	1 tsp.	5 mL
Crushed Ritz crackers (about 30 crackers)	1 cup	225 mL
Chopped pecans (or walnuts)	3/4 cup	175 mL

(continued on next page)

Frozen raspberries (or strawberries) in syrup, thawed	15 oz.	284 g
Whipping cream (see Tip, page 22)	1 cup	250 mL
Granulated sugar	2 tsp.	10 mL
Vanilla extract	1/2 tsp.	2 mL

Beat egg whites in large bowl until soft peaks form. Add sugar, 1 tbsp. (15 mL) at a time, beating constantly until stiff peaks form and sugar is dissolved. Add vanilla. Stir.

Fold in cracker crumbs and pecans. Spread in bottom and up side of greased 9 inch (22 cm) pie plate. Bake in 325°F (160°C) oven for about 30 minutes until golden. Let stand on wire rack to cool.

Spread raspberries and syrup over crust.

Beat cream, sugar and vanilla in small bowl until stiff peaks form. Spoon over raspberries. Let stand for at least 2 hours before cutting. Cuts into 8 wedges.

1 wedge: 435 Calories; 21.8 g Total Fat (9.8 g Mono, 3.0 g Poly, 8.0 g Sat); 41 mg Cholesterol; 58 g Carbohydrate; 3 g Fibre; 4 g Protein; 138 mg Sodium

Pictured below.

Left: Cranberry Pear Pie, page 62
Right: Berry Angel Pie, page 62

Sweet filling that's loaded with pecans—a delight to serve anytime.

Pecan Tart  *A Classic!*

Pastry for 1 crust 9 inch (22 cm) pie

Large eggs	4	4
Brown sugar, packed	1 cup	250 mL
Golden corn syrup	2/3 cup	150 mL
Butter (or hard margarine), melted	1/4 cup	60 mL
Grated orange zest	1 tsp.	5 mL
Vanilla extract	1 tsp.	5 mL
Salt	1/4 tsp.	1 mL
Chopped pecans, toasted (see Tip, page 9)	2 cups	500 mL
Pecan halves	16	16

Roll out pastry on lightly floured surface to about 1/8 inch (3 mm) thickness. Press in bottom and up side of 9 inch (22 cm) tart pan with fluted side and removable bottom. Trim edge. Cover. Chill for 30 minutes.

Beat eggs in large bowl until frothy. Add next 6 ingredients. Beat well.

Place tart pan on ungreased baking sheet (see Tip, page 40). Sprinkle chopped pecans over pastry. Spread egg mixture over pecans.

Arrange pecan halves around inside edge of crust. Bake on bottom rack in 400°F (205°C) oven for 10 minutes. Reduce heat to 350°F (175°C). Bake for about 35 minutes until filling is set and pastry is golden. Let stand in pan on wire rack to cool completely. Remove side of pan. Cuts into 8 wedges.

1 wedge: 613 Calories; 38.4 g Total Fat (14.7 g Mono, 7.3 g Poly, 9.4 g Sat); 128 mg Cholesterol; 66 g Carbohydrate; 3 g Fibre; 7 g Protein; 273 mg Sodium

Pictured at right.

A cream cheese layer hidden under a sweet, nutty layer. Cream cheese cuts the sweetness of this traditionally rich pie.

Two-Layer Pecan Pie

Pastry for 9 inch (22 cm) pie shell

Large egg	1	1
Cream cheese, softened	8 oz.	250 g
Granulated sugar	1/3 cup	75 mL
Vanilla extract	1 tsp.	5 mL

(continued on next page)

Large eggs	2	2
Corn syrup	2/3 cup	150 mL
Granulated sugar	1/3 cup	75 mL
All-purpose flour	1 tbsp.	15 mL
Vanilla extract	1 tsp.	5 mL
Chopped pecans	1 cup	250 mL

Roll out pastry on lightly floured surface to about 1/8 inch (3 mm) thickness. Press in bottom and up side of 9 inch (22 cm) pie plate. Trim, leaving 1/2 inch (12 mm) overhang. Roll under and crimp decorative edge. Cover pastry with parchment paper, bringing paper up over crimped edge. Fill halfway up side with dried beans. Bake on bottom rack in 375°F (190°C) oven for 15 minutes. Carefully remove beans and paper for the next time you bake pastry. Let pie shell stand on wire rack until cool.

Beat next 4 ingredients in medium bowl until smooth. Spread in pie shell.

Beat second amount of eggs in separate medium bowl until frothy. Add next 4 ingredients. Beat until smooth.

Stir in pecans. Spread over cream cheese layer. Bake on bottom rack in 350°F (175°C) oven for about 50 minutes until filling is evenly puffed and golden. Filling may still wobble in centre but will set upon cooling. Let stand on wire rack to cool completely. Cuts into 8 wedges.

1 wedge: 492 Calories; 28.8 g Total Fat (6.1 g Mono, 3.2 g Poly, 11.1 g Sat); 114 mg Cholesterol; 55 g Carbohydrate; 1 g Fibre; 7 g Protein; 261 mg Sodium

Pictured below.

Left: Two-Layer Pecan Pie, page 64
Right: Pecan Tart, page 64

Buttery moistness with lots of walnuts and coconut. A rich delight! Garnish individual servings with dollops of whipped cream, chocolate shavings and walnut pieces.

Chocolate-Crusted Walnut Pie

CHOCOLATE PIE CRUST

Package of pie crust mix (19 oz., 540 g, box)	1/2	1/2
Cocoa, sifted if lumpy	3 tbsp.	50 mL
Granulated sugar	3 tbsp.	50 mL
Cold water, approximately	1/4 cup	60 mL

FILLING

Golden corn syrup	1 cup	250 mL
Brown sugar, packed	3/4 cup	175 mL
Butter (or hard margarine)	2/3 cup	150 mL
Large eggs	3	3
Salt	1/8 tsp.	0.5 mL
Chopped walnuts, toasted (see Tip, page 9)	2 cups	500 mL
Medium unsweetened coconut, toasted (see Tip, page 9)	1 cup	250 mL
White vinegar	1 tbsp.	15 mL
Vanilla extract	1 1/2 tsp.	7 mL

Chocolate Pie Crust: Combine first 3 ingredients in medium bowl. Add water, 1 tbsp. (15 mL) at a time, stirring with fork until mixture starts to come together. Do not overmix. Turn out onto work surface. Shape into slightly flattened disc. Wrap with plastic wrap. Chill for 1 hour. Roll out between 2 sheets of waxed paper on dampened work surface to 12 inch (30 cm) circle (see Note 1). Discard top sheet of waxed paper. Line ungreased 9 inch (22 cm) deep dish pie plate with pastry, using waxed paper to help transfer (see Note 2). Discard waxed paper. Trim crust, leaving 1/2 inch (12 mm) overhang. Roll under and crimp decorative edge. Cover. Chill for 15 minutes.

Filling: Combine first 3 ingredients in medium saucepan on medium. Heat and stir for about 8 minutes until sugar is dissolved. Remove from heat. Let stand, stirring occasionally, until cooled to room temperature.

Beat eggs and salt in large bowl for about 5 minutes until thick and pale. Add corn syrup mixture. Beat well.

Add remaining 4 ingredients. Stir well. Spread in pie shell. Bake on bottom rack in 350°F (175°C) oven for about 50 minutes until golden and just set. Filling may still wobble in centre but will set upon cooling. Cuts into 10 wedges.

(continued on next page)

1 wedge: 641 Calories; 41.5 g Total Fat (10.5 g Mono, 13 g Poly, 15.4 g Sat); 75 mg Cholesterol;
66 g Carbohydrate; 3 g Fibre; 8 g Protein; 308 mg Sodium

Pictured below.

Note 1: Roll out dough between 2 sheets of waxed paper instead of using flour,
which may discolour the dough.

Note 2: A 10 inch pie plate also works well for this recipe.

A lavish indulgence of caramel, chocolate and nuts. Despite the name, this pie disappears fast.

Turtle Pie

FILLING

Box of chocolate pudding powder (not instant), 6-serving size	1	1
Milk	2 cups	500 mL
Thick caramel (or butterscotch) ice cream topping	1/3 cup	75 mL
Graham cracker crust	1	1
Chopped pecans	2/3 cup	150 mL

TOPPING

Frozen whipped topping, thawed	1 1/2 cups	375 mL
Thick caramel (or butterscotch) ice cream topping	2 tbsp.	30 mL
Chopped pecans	2 tbsp.	30 mL

Filling: Combine pudding powder and milk in medium saucepan. Heat and stir on medium for about 10 minutes until boiling and thickened. Remove from heat. Let stand at room temperature for 20 minutes, stirring often until cooled slightly.

Spread ice cream topping in bottom of crust. Sprinkle with pecans. Spread pudding over pecans. Cover with plastic wrap directly on surface to prevent skin from forming. Chill for about 1 1/2 hours until set. Remove plastic wrap.

Topping: Spread whipped topping over filling. Drizzle with ice cream topping. Sprinkle with pecans. Cuts into 8 wedges.

1 wedge: 298 Calories; 17.4 g Total Fat (4.7 g Mono, 2.4 g Poly, 5.2 g Sat); 4 mg Cholesterol; 33 g Carbohydrate; 1 g Fibre; 4 g Protein; 190 mg Sodium

Pictured at right.

Classic brownie flavour served up in a tender pastry crust. Serve warm or cold —try it with ice cream, too.

fudge icing

Garnish your Brownie Pie with this quick, shiny, very tasty icing.

Semi-sweet chocolate chips	1 cup	250 mL
Sour cream	1 cup	250 mL

Heat chocolate chips and sour cream in medium saucepan over hot water, or on low, stirring constantly, until smooth. Cool to room temperature. Makes 1²⁄3 cups (400 mL).

1/2 tbsp. (7 mL): 40 Calories; 1 g Protein; 1.9 g Total Fat; 6 g Carbohydrate; 20 mg Sodium; trace Fibre

Brownie Pie

Butter (or hard margarine), softened	1/2 cup	125 mL
Brown sugar, packed	1 cup	250 mL
Large eggs	2	2
Vanilla extract	1 tsp.	5 mL
All-purpose flour	2/3 cup	150 mL
Chopped walnuts	1/2 cup	125 mL
Cocoa, sifted if lumpy	1/2 cup	125 mL
Salt	1/4 tsp.	1 mL
Unbaked 9 inch (22 cm) pie shell	1	1

Beat butter and brown sugar in large bowl until light and fluffy. Add eggs, 1 at a time, beating well after each addition. Add vanilla. Stir.

Add next 4 ingredients. Stir well.

Spread in pie shell. Bake on bottom rack in 350°F (175°C) oven for about 30-35 minutes until wooden pick inserted in centre comes out moist but not wet with batter. Let stand on wire rack for at least 10 minutes before serving. Cuts into 8 wedges.

1 wedge (without icing): 404 Calories; 20.0 g Total Fat (2.9 g Mono, 0.4 g Poly, 10.6 g Sat); 89 mg Cholesterol; 52 g Carbohydrate; 1 g Fibre; 5 g Protein; 280 mg Sodium

Pictured below.

Maple Syrup Pie

A superb pie that highlights Canada's premium maple syrup.

Large eggs	2	2
Brown sugar, packed	1 cup	250 mL
Maple syrup	1 cup	250 mL
Butter (or hard margarine), softened	3 tbsp.	50 mL
All-purpose flour	2 tbsp.	30 mL
Chopped walnuts	3/4 cup	175 mL
Vanilla extract	1 tsp.	5 mL
Unbaked 9 inch (22 cm) pie shell	1	1

Beat eggs in medium bowl until frothy. Add next 4 ingredients. Beat until smooth.

Add walnuts and vanilla. Stir well.

Spread in pie shell. Bake on bottom rack in 375°F (190°C) oven for about 40 minutes until filling is golden and set. Let stand on wire rack until cooled completely. Cuts into 8 wedges.

1 wedge: 465 Calories; 19.8 g Total Fat (2.1 g Mono, 5.5 g Poly, 6.8 g Sat); 70 mg Cholesterol; 70 g Carbohydrate; 1 g Fibre; 4 g Protein; 161 mg Sodium

Pictured below.

A prize belonging to Kentucky. This has a cake-like topping over a delicious chocolate layer. Serve with whipped cream or ice cream.

about bourbon

Bourbon is an American whiskey made from fermented corn mash that is either sweet or sour and aged for a minimum of two years. It takes its name from Bourbon County in the state of Kentucky, where most bourbon is still made. A very fine, well-aged bourbon tastes similar to brandy and can replace it in recipes.

Kentucky Derby Pie

Butter (or hard margarine), softened	1/2 cup	125 mL
Granulated sugar	1 cup	250 mL
Large eggs	2	2
All-purpose flour	1/2 cup	125 mL
Bourbon whiskey	1 tbsp.	15 mL
Vanilla extract	1 1/2 tsp.	7 mL
Salt	1/4 tsp.	1 mL
Chopped pecans	1 cup	250 mL
Semi-sweet chocolate chips	1 cup	250 mL
Unbaked 9 inch (22 cm) pie shell	1	1

Whipped cream, for garnish
Sliced strawberries, for garnish

Beat butter and sugar in large bowl until light and fluffy. Add eggs, 1 at a time, beating well after each addition.

Add next 4 ingredients. Beat until smooth. Stir in nuts and chocolate chips.

Spread in pie shell. Bake on bottom rack in 350°F (180°C) oven for about 50 minutes until wooden pick inserted in centre comes out clean. Let stand on wire rack until cool.

Garnish with whipped cream and strawberries. Cuts into 8 wedges.

1 wedge: 572 Calories; 36.7 g Total Fat (11.2 g Mono, 3.9 g Poly, 15.3 g Sat); 89 mg Cholesterol; 60 g Carbohydrate; 3 g Fibre; 6 g Protein; 272 mg Sodium

Pictured at right.

Chocolate and peanut butter make a great pair in this chilled pie that kids of all ages will love.

Creamy Peanut Butter Pie

CHOCOLATE PEANUT CRUST

Butter (or hard margarine)	1/3 cup	75 mL
Chocolate wafer crumbs	2 cups	500 mL
Crunchy peanut butter	1/4 cup	60 mL
Icing (confectioner's) sugar	1 tbsp.	15 mL

PEANUT BUTTER FILLING

Granulated sugar	2/3 cup	150 mL
All-purpose flour	3 tbsp.	50 mL
Cornstarch	3 tbsp.	50 mL
Salt	1/2 tsp.	2 mL

(continued on next page)

Large eggs, fork-beaten	2	2
Milk	3 cups	750 mL
Butter (or hard margarine)	2 tbsp.	30 mL
Crunchy peanut butter	1/4 cup	60 mL
Vanilla extract	1 tsp.	5 mL
Frozen whipped topping, thawed	2 cups	500 mL

Chocolate Peanut Crust: Melt butter in medium saucepan. Remove from heat. Add next 3 ingredients. Stir until well mixed. Reserve 3 tbsp. (50 mL) crumb mixture in small cup. Press remaining crumb mixture firmly in bottom and up side of 9 inch (22 cm) deep dish pie plate. Bake in 350°F (175°C) oven for 10 minutes. Let stand on wire rack to cool.

Peanut Butter Filling: Combine first 4 ingredients in large saucepan.

Add next 3 ingredients. Stir. Heat and stir on medium until mixture comes to a boil and thickens. Remove from heat.

Add peanut butter and vanilla. Stir well. Cool to room temperature. Spread in crust. Chill for at least 2 hours until set.

Spread whipped topping over filling. Sprinkle with reserved crumbs. Cuts into 8 wedges.

1 wedge: 507 Calories; 28.4 g Total Fat (4.4 g Mono, 1.6 g Poly, 14.2 g Sat); 88 mg Cholesterol; 55 g Carbohydrate; 2 g Fibre; 11 g Protein; 522 mg Sodium

Pictured below

Top: Creamy Peanut Butter Pie, page 72
Bottom: Kentucky Derby Pie, page 72

A moist, cake-like filling tops a rich, buttery crust. Serve cold or at room temperature.

Almond Rhubarb Tart

BUTTER CRUST

Butter (or hard margarine), softened	1/2 cup	125 mL
Granulated sugar	1/4 cup	60 mL
Large egg	1	1
All-purpose flour	1 1/3 cups	325 mL
Salt	1/4 tsp.	1 mL

RHUBARB FILLING

Strawberry jam, warmed	1/4 cup	60 mL
Butter (or hard margarine), softened	1/2 cup	125 mL
Granulated sugar	1/2 cup	125 mL
Vanilla extract	1 tsp.	5 mL
Large eggs	2	2
Frozen rhubarb, thawed and drained	1 cup	250 mL
Ground almonds	3/4 cup	175 mL

TOPPING

Sliced almonds	1/3 cup	75 mL
Apricot jam, warmed and sieved	2 tbsp.	30 mL

Butter Crust: Beat butter and sugar in medium bowl until combined. Add egg. Beat well.

Add flour and salt. Stir until mixture starts to come together. Do not overmix. Turn out onto work surface. Shape into slightly flattened disc. Wrap with plastic wrap. Chill for 30 minutes. Roll out pastry on lightly floured surface to fit ungreased 8 inch (20 cm), deep tart pan with removable bottom (see Note). Carefully lift pastry and press in bottom and up side of pan. Trim edge. Place pan on ungreased baking sheet (see Tip, page 40). Cover. Chill for 1 hour.

Rhubarb Filling: Spread strawberry jam over bottom of crust.

Beat butter, sugar and vanilla in medium bowl until light and creamy. Add eggs, 1 at a time, beating well after each addition. Stir in rhubarb and ground almonds. Spread over jam layer.

Topping: Sprinkle with sliced almonds. Bake on bottom rack in 350°F (175°C) oven for 40 to 45 minutes until filling is set and crust is golden. Let stand in pan on wire rack for 10 minutes.

Carefully brush tart with apricot jam. Cool. Chill at least 6 hours or overnight. Cuts into 8 wedges.

1 wedge: 486 Calories; 31.2 g Total Fat (10.2 g Mono, 2.5 g Poly, 15.5 g Sat); 141 mg Cholesterol; 47 g Carbohydrate; 2 g Fibre; 7 g Protein; 261 mg Sodium

(continued on next page)

Pictured on page 77.

Note: If you don't have a deep tart pan, a regular 8 inch (20 cm) tart pan will also work.

Peach And Almond Tart

A tempting blend of peaches and almonds with a warm cinnamon aroma.

ALMOND PASTRY

All-purpose flour	1 1/4 cups	300 mL
Cold butter (or hard margarine), cut up	1/3 cup	75 mL
Icing (confectioner's) sugar	1/3 cup	75 mL
Ground almonds	1/4 cup	60 mL
Egg yolks (large)	2	2
Ice water, approximately	2 tbsp.	30 mL

PEACH ALMOND FILLING

Ground almonds, toasted (see Tip, page 9)	1/2 cup	125 mL
Cans of sliced peaches (14 oz., 398 mL, each), drained	2	2
Brown sugar, packed	1/3 cup	75 mL
Slivered almonds	1/4 cup	60 mL
Ground cinnamon	1/2 tsp.	2 mL

Almond Pastry: Process first 4 ingredients in food processor until mixture resembles coarse crumbs.

Add egg yolks and ice water. Pulse with on/off motion until mixture starts to come together. Do not over process. Turn out onto lightly floured surface. Form pastry into ball. Flatten slightly into disc. Wrap with plastic wrap. Chill for 30 minutes. Roll out pastry on lightly floured surface to 12 inch (30 cm) circle. Carefully transfer to greased 11 x 17 inch (28 x 43 cm) baking sheet.

Peach And Almond Filling: Sprinkle ground almonds over pastry, leaving 3 inch border. Arrange peach slices in single layer over almonds.

Combine next 3 ingredients in small cup. Sprinkle over peach slices. Fold a section of edge up and over edge of filling. Repeat with next section, allowing pastry to overlap so that fold is created. Repeat until pastry border is completely folded around filling. Bake on bottom rack in 375°F (190°C) oven for about 35 minutes until pastry is golden. Cuts into 8 wedges.

1 wedge: 345 Calories; 15.0 g Total Fat (6.4 g Mono, 2.0 g Poly, 5.7 g Sat); 71 mg Cholesterol; 50 g Carbohydrate; 4 g Fibre; 6 g Protein; 65 mg Sodium

Pictured on page 77.

A smooth, elegant chocolate tart with a hint of hazelnut in the crust. The perfect finish to a dinner party. For extra flavour, serve with Cinnamon Cream, below.

cinnamon cream

Whipping cream	2/3 cup	150 mL
Icing	2 tbsp.	30 mL
(confectioner's) sugar		
Ground cinnamon	1/4 tsp.	1 mL
Hazelnut-flavoured	2 tbsp.	30 mL
liqueur		

Beat first 3 ingredients in small bowl until soft peaks form.

Add liqueur. Stir until smooth. Makes 1 1/2 cups (375 mL) cream.

2 tbsp. (30 mL) Cinnamon Cream:
57 Calories; 4.7 g Total Fat (1.4 g Mono, 0.2 g Poly, 2.9 g Sat); 17 mg Cholesterol; 3 g Carbohydrate; trace Fibre; trace Protein; 5 mg Sodium

Blind Baking

Place sheet of parchment paper (or foil) over crust, bringing paper up over side of pan. Fill halfway up side with dried beans or rice. Bake in 375°F (190°C) oven for 15 minutes.

Rich Chocolate Tart

HAZELNUT PASTRY

All-purpose flour	1 cup	250 mL
Cold butter (or hard margarine), cut up	1/2 cup	125 mL
Finely ground hazelnuts (filberts)	1/3 cup	75 mL
Icing (confectioner's) sugar	1/3 cup	75 mL
Egg yolks (large)	2	2
Ice water	1 tbsp.	15 mL

CHOCOLATE FILLING

Whipping cream	1 cup	250 mL
Prepared strong coffee	1/4 cup	60 mL
Semi-sweet chocolate baking squares (1 oz., 28 g, each), chopped	16	16

Icing (confectioner's) sugar, for dusting

Hazelnut Pastry: Process first 4 ingredients in food processor until mixture resembles coarse crumbs. Add egg yolks and water. Pulse with on/off motion until mixture starts to come together. Do not over process. Turn out onto lightly floured surface. Flatten slightly into disc. Wrap with plastic wrap. Chill for 30 minutes. Roll out pastry to fit ungreased 10 inch (25 cm) tart pan with fluted sides and removable bottom. Carefully lift pastry and press in bottom and up side of pan. Trim edge. Place on ungreased baking sheet (see Tip, page 40). Cover. Chill for 1 hour. Cover pastry with parchment paper, bringing paper up over crimped edge. Fill halfway up side with dried beans. Bake on bottom rack in 375°F (190°C) oven for 15 minutes. Carefully remove beans and paper (these can be kept for the next time you bake pastry). Bake crust for about 10 minutes until lightly browned. Let stand on wire rack until cool.

Chocolate Filling: Heat whipping cream and coffee in medium saucepan on medium until bubbles appear around edge of pan. Add chocolate. Heat and stir on lowest heat for about 1 minute until chocolate is almost melted. Remove from heat. Stir until smooth. Cool for 30 minutes. Spread in crust. Chill at least 6 hours or overnight until set. Remove side of pan.

Dust with icing sugar (see Note). Cuts into 12 wedges.

Note: To dust top of tart decoratively, cut thick paper into 12 strips, 1/2 inch (12 mm) wide and 10 inches (25 cm) long. Arrange 6 strips in one direction, 1 inch (2.5 cm) apart, across tart. Repeat with remaining strips in opposite direction to form diamond shapes. Dust liberally with icing sugar. Carefully remove paper strips.

(continued on next page)

1 wedge (without cream): 397 Calories; 28.3 g Total Fat (5.9 g Mono, 0.9 g Poly, 16.4 g Sat); 81 mg Cholesterol; 36 g Carbohydrate; 2 g Fibre; 5 g Protein; 63 mg Sodium

Pictured below.

1. Rich Chocolate Tart, page 76
2. Peach And Almond Tart, page 75
3. Almond Rhubarb Tart, page 74

Bacon pieces give this creamy pie a striking appearance.

reheating instructions

Cover with foil. Bake in 400°F (205°C) oven for about 20 minutes until heated through.

Quiche Lorraine *A Classic!*

Grated Swiss cheese	1 cup	250 mL
Unbaked 9 inch (22 cm) pie shell	1	1
Bacon slices, cooked crisp and crumbled	12	12
Large eggs	4	4
Skim evaporated milk	1 3/4 cup	425 mL
Salt	1/2 tsp.	2 mL
Pepper	1/4 tsp.	1 mL
Ground nutmeg	1/8 tsp.	0.5 mL
Onion powder	1/8 tsp.	0.5 mL

Sprinkle cheese in pie shell. Scatter bacon over cheese.

Beat eggs in medium bowl. Add next 5 ingredients. Beat well. Pour into shell. Bake on bottom rack in 350°F (175°C) oven for about 45 minutes until knife inserted in centre comes out clean. Let stand on wire rack for 10 minutes before serving. Cuts into 6 wedges.

1 wedge: 443 Calories; 27.6 g Total Fat (3.3 g Mono, 0.8 g Poly, 13.6 g Sat); 204 mg Cholesterol; 26 g Carbohydrate; trace Fibre; 19 g Protein; 773 mg Sodium

Pictured at right.

A full-meal deal with lots of flavour.

Chicken Quiche

Cooking oil	1 tbsp.	15 mL
Boneless, skinless chicken breast halves (about 2), diced	1/2 lb.	225 g
Medium onion, chopped	1	1
Cauliflower florets	1 1/2 cups	375 mL
Water	1/4 cup	60 mL
Grated light sharp Cheddar cheese	1/2 cup	125 mL
Unbaked 9 inch (22 cm) pie shell	1	1
Large eggs	3	3
All-purpose flour	1 tbsp.	15 mL
Skim evaporated milk	2/3 cup	150 mL
Salt	3/4 tsp.	4 mL
Pepper	1/4 tsp.	1 mL
Ground nutmeg, just a pinch		
Green onions, chopped	2	2

(continued on next page)

Heat cooking oil in medium frying pan on medium. Add chicken and onion. Cook for 5 to 10 minutes, stirring occasionally until golden.

Add cauliflower and water. Cover. Steam for about 4 minutes until cauliflower is tender-crisp. Remove cover. Heat and stir until water has evaporated. Remove from heat. Cool.

Sprinkle cheese in bottom of pie shell. Spoon chicken mixture over top.

Beat eggs and flour in medium bowl until smooth. Add next 4 ingredients. Beat well. Pour over chicken.

Sprinkle with green onion. Bake on bottom rack in 350°F (175°C) oven for about 40 minutes until knife inserted in centre comes out clean. Let stand on wire rack for 10 minutes before serving. Cuts into 6 wedges.

1 wedge: 314 Calories; 15.9 g Total Fat (1.8 g Mono, 1.0 g Poly, 6.0 g Sat); 105 mg Cholesterol; 26 g Carbohydrate; 1 g Fibre; 17 g Protein; 566 mg Sodium

Pictured below.

Left: Chicken Quiche, page 78
Right: Quiche Lorraine, page 78

A beautiful quiche with just the right amount of warm, rich flavour.

how to roast your own peppers

All you'll need to roast your own red bell peppers is your oven's broiler and the following steps:

1. Put peppers on an ungreased baking sheet and broil 4 inches (10 cm) from the element for about 10 minutes. Turn peppers often until all sides are blackened.

2. Put the peppers in a large bowl and cover with plastic wrap. Let sweat for about 15 minutes so the steam can loosen the charred skin.

3. Peel off skin. Remove the seeds and ribs from the inside.

4. Enjoy anywhere you'd use roasted red peppers!

about liquid smoke

What's liquid smoke? This oddly named additive is actually made from the condensed vapours of wet, burning hickory wood chips mixed with water and then processed to remove any tar or ash. It is used to give a variety of dishes the smoky flavour of food grilled over a wood fire; some say it imparts the taste of smoked bacon and the aroma of a campfire. Good quality liquid smoke should be a reddish gold colour, should contain no additives or colourants and should have little to no visible sediment in the bottle.

Beef And Rice Quiche

Large egg	1	1
Warm cooked long grain white rice	2 cups	500 mL
Chopped chives	2 tbsp.	30 mL
Large eggs, fork-beaten	3	3
Can of skim evaporated milk	13 1/2 oz.	385 mL
Finely chopped cooked lean beef	1 cup	250 mL
Grated medium Cheddar cheese	1 cup	250 mL
Sliced green onion	1/2 cup	125 mL
Chopped fresh parsley (or 3/4 tsp., 4 mL, flakes)	1 tbsp.	15 mL
Dry mustard	1/2 tsp.	2 mL
Liquid smoke (optional)	1/2 tsp.	2 mL
Salt	1/2 tsp.	2 mL
Medium roasted red pepper (see Sidebar), cut into 8 strips	1	1

Combine first 3 ingredients in small bowl. Press mixture firmly in bottom and up sides of greased 9 inch (22 cm) deep dish pie plate to form crust. Bake in 350°F (175°C) oven for 5 minutes.

Combine next 9 ingredients in large bowl. Pour into rice crust.

Arrange red pepper in pinwheel design on top. Bake, uncovered, in 350°F (175°C) oven for 45 minutes until knife inserted in centre comes out clean. Immediately run knife around inside edge to loosen crust. Let stand on wire rack for 10 minutes before serving. Cuts into 8 wedges.

1 wedge: 236 Calories; 9.9 g Total Fat (1.4 g Mono, 0.2 g Poly, 4.9 g Sat); 141 mg Cholesterol; 19 g Carbohydrate; trace Fibre; 16 g Protein; 345 mg Sodium

Pictured on page 83.

Leek-Crowned Beef Pie

Butter (or hard margarine)	1 tbsp.	15 mL
Thinly sliced leeks (white part only)	2 cups	500 mL
Large eggs, fork-beaten	3	3
Homogenized milk	1/2 cup	125 mL

(continued on next page)

Grated Parmesan cheese	1/4 cup	60 mL
Salt, sprinkle		
Pepper, sprinkle		
Cooking oil	2 tsp.	10 mL
Italian sausages, casings removed, chopped	1/2 lb.	225 g
Lean ground beef	1/2 lb.	225 g
Chopped onion	1 cup	250 mL
Garlic cloves, minced (or 1/2 tsp., 2 mL, powder)	2	2
Can of condensed cream of mushroom soup	10 oz.	284 mL
Dried basil	1/2 tsp.	2 mL
Dried oregano	1/2 tsp.	2 mL

Pastry for 9 inch (22 cm) deep dish pie

Melt butter in large frying pan on medium. Add leek. Cook for about 5 minutes, stirring often, until softened. Transfer to medium bowl.

Add next 5 ingredients to leek mixture. Stir. Set aside.

Heat cooking oil in same pan on medium. Add sausage and ground beef. Scramble-fry for about 10 minutes until no longer pink. Transfer with slotted spoon to separate medium bowl. Set aside.

Drain drippings from pan. Heat same pan on medium. Add onion and garlic. Cook for 5 to 10 minutes, stirring often, until onion is softened.

Add next 3 ingredients and beef mixture. Heat and stir for 1 minute. Remove from heat. Cool slightly.

Roll out pastry on lightly floured surface to about 1/8 inch (3 mm) thickness. Line 9 inch (22 cm) deep dish pie plate. Trim pastry, leaving 1/2 inch (12 mm) overhang. Roll under and crimp decorative edge. Spread beef mixture in shell. Pour leek mixture over top. Bake on bottom rack in 400°F (205°C) oven for 15 minutes. Reduce heat to 350°F (175°C). Bake for 35 to 40 minutes until knife inserted in centre comes out clean. Let stand on wire rack for 10 minutes before serving. Cuts into 6 wedges.

1 wedge: 421 Calories; 26.4 g Total Fat (3.9 g Mono, 1.3 g Poly, 10.1 g Sat); 166 mg Cholesterol; 27 g Carbohydrate; 1 g Fibre; 19 g Protein; 856 mg Sodium

Pictured on page 83.

Before it's cut, this main dish pie looks like a quiche. A rich leek and cheese layer rests atop a savoury beef and sausage combination.

about Italian sausage

Italian sausage is made of pork, typically flavoured with fennel or anise and garlic, and comes in two varieties: hot (with hot peppers) and mild or sweet (without hot peppers). It is not smoked or cured, so it must always be cooked before being eaten. It is readily available in supermarkets everywhere.

This deep dish pie has a thick, rich filling. Try it with Gouda or Monterey Jack cheese instead of Edam.

Chicken Broccoli Pie

Lean ground chicken	1 lb.	454 g
Finely chopped celery	1/4 cup	60 mL
Finely chopped onion	1/4 cup	60 mL
All-purpose flour	2 tbsp.	30 mL
Salt	1/2 tsp.	2 mL
Pepper	1/8 tsp.	0.5 mL
Garlic powder	1/8 tsp.	0.5 mL
Milk	1 1/4 cups	300 mL
Herb-flavoured cream cheese	1/2 cup	125 mL
Large egg, fork-beaten	1	1
Chopped fresh (or frozen) broccoli, cooked and drained	4 cups	1 L
Grated Edam cheese	1 cup	250 mL
Pastry for 2 crust 9 inch (25 cm) deep dish pie		
Milk	1 tbsp.	15 mL

Scramble-fry first 3 ingredients in large non-stick frying pan on medium until onion is soft and chicken is no longer pink.

Add next 4 ingredients. Stir well. Slowly add milk, stirring until mixture is boiling and thickened. Remove from heat.

Stir in cream cheese until melted.

Add next 3 ingredients. Stir.

Divide pastry into 2 portions, making 1 portion slightly larger than the other. Shape each portion into slightly flattened disc. Roll out larger portion on lightly floured surface to about 1/8 inch (3 mm) thickness. Line 9 inch (22 cm) deep dish pie plate. Spread chicken mixture in shell. Roll out smaller portion on lightly floured surface to about 1/8 inch (3 mm) thickness. Dampen edge of pastry shell with water. Cover with remaining pastry. Trim and crimp decorative edge to seal.

Brush top of pie with milk. Cut several small vents in top to allow steam to escape. Bake on bottom rack in 350°F (175°C) oven for 45 to 50 minutes until golden (see Tip, page 42). Let stand on wire rack for 10 minutes before serving. Cuts into 6 wedges.

1 wedge: 583 Calories; 36.0 g Total Fat (3.3 g Mono, 0.3 g Poly, 17.3 g Sat); 159 mg Cholesterol; 36 g Carbohydrate; 2 g Fibre; 30 g Protein; 975 mg Sodium

Pictured at right.

1. Leek-Crowned Beef Pie, page 80
2. Chicken Broccoli Pie, page 82
3. Beef And Rice Quiche, page 80

A moist and tasty chicken pie that cuts into beautiful wedges. Treat your friends or family to this outstanding, savoury dish.

about leeks

Leeks look like large green onions and are related to both onions and garlic, but their flavour is milder. When buying leeks, choose smaller ones with fresh-looking, dark green leaves and clean, blemish-free white stalks. Large leeks are generally less flavourful than smaller ones. Always discard the root and green leaves before cooking, and always wash them well by slicing the white parts down the centre lengthwise, from top to bottom, and rinsing out any dirt trapped between the layers.

tip

Don't have any leftover chicken? Start with 3 boneless, skinless chicken breast halves (about 1 lb., 454g). Place in a large frying pan with 1 cup (250 mL) water or chicken broth. Simmer, covered, for 12 to14 minutes until no longer pink inside. Chop. Makes about 3 cups (750 mL) of cooked chicken.

Chick And Leek Pie

Butter (or hard margarine)	2 tbsp.	30 mL
Thinly sliced leeks (white part only)	2 cups	500 mL
Brown sugar, packed	2 tsp.	10 mL
Finely chopped carrot	1 cup	250 mL
Finely chopped celery	1/2 cup	125 mL
Garlic cloves, minced (or 3/4 tsp., 4 mL, powder)	3	3
Salt	1/4 tsp.	1 mL
Pepper	1/8 tsp.	0.5 mL
All-purpose flour	2 tbsp.	30 mL
Prepared chicken broth	1 cup	250 mL
Dry (or alcohol-free) white wine	1/4 cup	60 mL
Chopped cooked chicken (see Tip)	3 cups	750 mL
Sour cream	1/4 cup	60 mL
Pastry for 2 crust 9 inch (22 cm) pie		
Large egg, fork-beaten	1	1

Melt butter in large frying pan on medium-low. Add leek. Cook for 15 to 20 minutes, stirring often, until caramelized.

Add next 6 ingredients. Heat and stir for about 5 minutes until carrot and celery are softened. Increase heat to medium.

Add flour. Heat and stir for 1 minute. Slowly add broth and wine, stirring constantly for 5 to 7 minutes until boiling and thickened.

Add chicken and sour cream. Stir well. Remove from heat. Cool.

Divide pastry into 2 portions, 1 slightly larger than the other. Roll out larger portion on lightly floured surface to about 1/8 inch (3 mm) thickness. Line 9 inch (22 cm) pie plate. Spread chicken mixture in pie shell. Roll out smaller portion on lightly floured surface to about 1/8 inch (3 mm) thickness.

Brush edge of pie shell with egg. Cover with remaining pastry. Trim and crimp decorative edge to seal. Brush top of pie with remaining egg. Cut several small vents in top to allow steam to escape. Bake on bottom rack in 375°F (190°C) oven for about 50 minutes until golden (see Tip, page 42). Let stand on wire rack for 10 minutes before serving. Cuts into 6 wedges.

1 wedge: 595 Calories; 31.6 g Total Fat (3.4 g Mono, 1.8 g Poly, 13.6 g Sat); 132 mg Cholesterol; 47 g Carbohydrate; 1 g Fibre; 27 g Protein; 746 mg Sodium

Pictured at right.

1. Cheeseburger Pie, page 86
2. Chick And Leek Pie, page 84

Savoury pie that tastes just like a gourmet cheeseburger! Hearty and satisfying.

Cheeseburger Pie

Extra-lean ground beef	12 oz.	340 g
Chopped onion	3/4 cup	175 mL
Garlic clove, minced (or 1/4 tsp., 1 mL, powder), optional	1	1
Grated sharp Cheddar cheese	1/2 cup	125 mL
Unbaked 9 inch (22 cm) pie shell	1	1
Large eggs	3	3
Skim evaporated milk	1 cup	250 mL
Grated sharp Cheddar cheese	3/4 cup	175 mL
Beef bouillon powder	1/2 tsp.	2 mL
Salt	1/2 tsp.	2 mL
Pepper	1/4 tsp.	1 mL
Medium tomato, cut into 6 slices	1	1
Dried oregano, sprinkle		

Scramble-fry first 3 ingredients in large non-stick frying pan on medium for about 10 minutes until beef is no longer pink. Remove from heat. Cool.

Sprinkle first amount of cheese in bottom of pie shell. Spread beef mixture over top.

Whisk eggs in large bowl until smooth. Add next 5 ingredients. Stir well. Pour over beef mixture.

Arrange tomato slices on top. Sprinkle with oregano. Bake on bottom rack in 425°F (220°C) oven for 10 minutes. Reduce heat to 350°F (175°C). Bake for about 50 minutes until knife inserted in centre comes out clean. Let stand on wire rack for 10 minutes before serving. Cuts into 6 wedges.

1 wedge: 403 Calories; 21.8 g Total Fat (3.2 g Mono, 0.5 g Poly, 10.5 g Sat); 169 mg Cholesterol; 27 g Carbohydrate; trace Fibre; 24 g Protein; 683 mg Sodium

Pictured on page 85.

Rich pastry encloses a filling of creamy beef and vegetables.

Beef And Vegetable Pie

Cooking oil	2 tsp.	10 mL
Lean ground beef	1 lb.	454 g
Frozen mixed vegetables (large pieces halved)	2 cups	500mL
Can of condensed cream of mushroom soup	10 oz.	284 mL
Beef bouillon powder	1 tsp.	5 mL

(continued on next page)

Onion powder	1/2 tsp.	2 mL
Pepper	1/4 tsp.	1 mL

Pastry for 2 crust 9 inch (22 cm) pie

Heat cooking oil in large frying pan on medium. Add ground beef. Scramble-fry for about 10 minutes until no longer pink. Drain. Transfer to medium bowl. Cool.

Add next 5 ingredients. Stir.

Divide pastry into 2 portions, making 1 portion slightly larger than the other. Shape each portion into slightly flattened disc. Roll out larger portion on lightly floured surface to about 1/8 inch (3 mm) thickness. Line 9 inch (22 cm) pie plate. Spread beef mixture in shell. Roll out smaller portion on lightly floured surface to about 1/8 inch (3 mm) thickness. Dampen edge of pastry shell with water. Cover with remaining pastry. Trim and crimp decorative edge to seal. Cut several small vents in top to allow steam to escape. Bake on bottom rack in 400°F (205°C) oven for 15 minutes. Reduce heat to 350°F (175°C). Bake for 35 to 40 minutes until golden (see Tip, page 42). Let stand on wire rack for 10 minutes before serving. Cuts into 6 wedges.

1 wedge: 217 Calories; 13.6 g Total Fat (0.9 g Mono, 0.5 g Poly, 4.6 g Sat); 54 mg Cholesterol; 7 g Carbohydrate; 1 g Fibre; 16 g Protein; 636 mg Sodium

Pictured below.

Beef And Vegetable Pie, page 86

A taste of tradition with simmered beef, kidney and onions in a rich sauce beneath a golden pastry crust. Reserve this hearty, comforting English specialty for cold days.

tip

To allow steam to escape and reduce likelihood of gravy splashing onto pastry top, make a "chimney." Cut a 6 x 12 inch (15 x 30 cm) piece of foil. Fold into 2 x 12 inch (5 x 30 cm) strip. Roll foil strip around 3/4 inch (2 cm) diameter wooden spoon handle or dowel to make 2 inch (5 cm) high cylinder.

Steak And Kidney Pie

FILLING

Round steak, cut into 1 inch (2.5 cm) cubes	2 lbs.	900 g
All-purpose flour	1/4 cup	60 mL
Salt	1/2 tsp.	2 mL
Pepper	1/2 tsp.	2 mL
Cooking oil	2 tbsp.	15 mL
Medium onions, coarsely chopped	3	3
Prepared beef broth	2 cups	500 mL
Bay leaves	2	2
Fresh beef kidney (see Note)	1 lb.	454 g
Cooking oil	2 tbsp.	30 mL

PASTRY

All-purpose flour	1 1/2 cups	375 mL
Salt	1/2 tsp.	2 mL
Cold lard (or shortening), cut up	3/4 cup	175 mL
Egg yolks (large)	2	2
Cold water, approximately	2 tbsp.	30 mL
White vinegar	1/2 tsp.	2 mL
Large egg	1	1
Milk	1 tbsp.	15 mL

Filling: Combine first 4 ingredients in resealable freezer bag. Shake until coated. Remove beef cubes from flour. Reserve remaining flour mixture.

Heat 1 tbsp. (15 mL) of cooking oil in Dutch oven on medium-high. Add 1/2 of beef. Cook for about 5 minutes, stirring often until browned. Remove from pan. Repeat with remaining cooking oil and beef.

Add onion to same pan. Cook on medium-high for about 5 minutes, stirring often until softened. Add reserved flour mixture. Heat and stir for 1 minute.

Gradually stir broth into onion mixture until smooth. Add beef and bay leaves. Bring to a boil. Reduce heat to medium-low. Cover. Simmer for 1 hour, stirring occasionally, until beef is tender. Remove and discard bay leaves. Remove beef and onion with slotted spoon to large bowl. Boil liquid, uncovered, in same pan until reduced to 1 cup (250 mL). Add to beef mixture.

(continued on next page)

Trim kidney of fat and veins. Cut into 3/4 inch (2 cm) cubes. Heat second amount of cooking oil in large frying pan on medium. Add kidney. Cook for about 3 minutes, stirring occasionally until lightly browned. Add to beef mixture. Stir. Set filling aside.

Pastry: Combine flour and salt in medium bowl. Cut in lard until mixture resembles coarse crumbs.

Whisk next 3 ingredients in small bowl. Add to flour mixture. Mix until soft dough forms. Shape into flattened ball. Wrap with plastic wrap. Chill for 15 minutes. Roll out pastry on lightly floured surface to 1/8 inch (3 mm) thickness. Cut out 10 inch (25 cm) circle. Set aside. Roll out pastry trimmings to 1/8 inch (3 mm) thickness. Cut into 1 inch (2.5 cm) wide strips. Dampen and press ends of strips together to make 1 strip long enough to circle rim of 9 inch (22 cm) pie plate. Fold and press strip over rim of pie plate. Roll out remaining pastry trimmings to 1/8 inch (3 mm) thickness. Cut into leaves or shapes to decorate pie top. Set aside. Pour filling into pie plate.

Whisk egg and milk together in small cup. Brush over top of pastry strip. Place pastry circle on top. Crimp decorative edge to seal. Make 3/4 inch (2 cm) hole in centre of pie. Insert chimney (see Tip), leaving about 1/2 inch (12 mm) protruding. Decorate top of pie with reserved pastry shapes. Brush with egg mixture. Bake in 375°F (190°C) oven for 30 to 35 minutes until flaky and deep golden. Let stand on wire rack for 10 minutes. Remove chimney. Cuts into 8 wedges.

1 wedge: 721 Calories; 38.8 g Total Fat (17.7 g Mono, 4.7 g Poly, 12.8 g Sat); 439 mg Cholesterol; 24 g Carbohydrate; 1 g Fibre; 65 g Protein; 821 mg Sodium

Pictured on page 91.

Note: For a less pronounced kidney taste, soak whole kidneys overnight, in refrigerator, in lightly salted water or milk.

A French Canadian favourite—this recipe makes two deliciously seasoned pork and potato pies. Bon appétit!

Tourtière is a meat pie whose origins date back to 17th-century Quebec. It's a festive dish served at Christmas or on New Year's Eve (Rèveillon). There are as many recipes for this dish as there are regions of Quebec, and the ingredients in the pie can vary depending on location and availability. The most common recipe uses ground pork or a mix of ground pork, beef and veal. Some recipes use cubed meat. Fish, seafood or wild game are possible substitutions. Cinnamon, cloves, nutmeg and allspice are the traditional seasonings, but the use of savoury, rosemary and other herbs have been recorded. Versions of the dish influenced by Irish cooking also include rolled oats and potatoes as thickeners.

Pork Tourtière

Lean ground pork	2 lbs.	900 g
Finely chopped onion	1 1/2 cups	375 mL
Water	1 cup	250 mL
Salt	1 tsp.	5 mL
Pepper	1/2 tsp.	2 mL
Poultry seasoning	1/2 tsp.	2 mL
Garlic powder	1/4 tsp.	1 mL
Bay leaf	1	1
Ground cloves	1/8 tsp.	0.5 mL
Cooked mashed potato	2 cups	500 mL
Large egg, fork-beaten	1	1
Water	1 tbsp.	15 mL
Unbaked 9 inch (22 cm) pie shells	4	4

Combine first 9 ingredients in large saucepan or Dutch oven. Bring to a boil. Reduce heat to medium. Simmer, uncovered, for about 15 minutes, stirring occasionally, until pork is no longer pink and liquid has been reduced by half. Remove and discard bay leaf.

Add potato. Stir. Mixture should be moist and thick. Remove from heat. Cool completely.

Combine egg and water in small bowl. Brush edges of 2 pie shells with egg mixture. Spread potato mixture in shells. Roll out remaining pie shells to fit over top. Crimp decorative edge to seal. Brush with egg mixture. Cut several small vents in top to allow steam to escape. Bake on bottom rack in 375°F (190°C) oven for about 50 minutes until golden (see Tip, page 42). Let stand on wire racks for 10 minutes before serving. Makes 2 pies, each cut into 6 wedges, for a total of 12 wedges.

1 wedge: 528 Calories; 30.7 g Total Fat (5.1 g Mono, 1.1 g Poly, 12.5 g Sat); 83 mg Cholesterol; 43 g Carbohydrate; trace Fibre; 18 g Protein; 597 mg Sodium

Pictured at right.

Top: Steak And Kidney Pie, page 88
Bottom: Pork Tourtière, above

This traditional-looking quiche tastes like fresh pizza. Serve either warm or cold for lunch or snack time.

Pepper And Ham Quiche

Pastry for 9 inch (22 cm) pie shell

Cooking oil	1 tbsp.	15 mL
Thinly sliced onion	1/2 cup	125 mL
Chopped green pepper	1/2 cup	125 mL
Chopped red pepper	1/2 cup	125 mL
Chopped cooked ham (about 4 1/2 oz., 127 g)	3/4 cup	175 mL
Grated Gruyère cheese	1/2 cup	125 mL
Large eggs	3	3
Milk	1 cup	250 mL
Sour cream	1/4 cup	60 mL
Pepper	1/4 tsp.	1 mL

Roll out pastry on lightly floured surface to 1/8 inch (3 mm) thickness. Line 9 inch (22 cm) pie plate. Trim, leaving 1/2 inch (12 mm) overhang. Roll under and crimp decorative edge.

Heat cooking oil in medium frying pan on medium. Add onion. Cook for 5 to 10 minutes, stirring often, until onion is softened.

Add green and red peppers. Cook for about 3 minutes, stirring occasionally until peppers are softened. Remove from heat. Cool.

Sprinkle, ham, cheese and onion mixture over bottom of pie shell.

Whisk remaining 4 ingredients in medium bowl. Carefully pour over ham mixture. Bake on bottom rack in 350°F (175°C) oven for 50 to 60 minutes until knife inserted in centre comes out clean. Let stand on wire rack for 10 minutes before serving. Cuts into 6 wedges.

1 wedge: 319 Calories; 19.5 g Total Fat (2.4 g Mono, 0.9 g Poly, 8.2 g Sat); 143 mg Cholesterol; 22 g Carbohydrate; trace Fibre; 12 g Protein; 375 mg Sodium

Pictured on page 3 and at right.

A golden, flaky crust with a rich, creamy shrimp filling. Delicious!

Shrimp Quiche

Pastry for 10 inch (25 cm) pie shell

Cooked shrimp, coarsely chopped	1 1/2 cups	375 mL
Cream cheese, cut into small pieces	4 oz.	125 g

(continued on next page)

Large eggs	6	6
Whipping cream	2 cups	500 mL
Chopped fresh dill	2 tsp.	10 mL
(or 1/2 tsp., 2 mL, dill weed)		
Salt	1/4 tsp.	1 mL
Pepper, just a pinch		

Roll out pastry on lightly floured surface to fit ungreased 10 inch (25 cm) tart pan with fluted sides and removable bottom. Carefully lift pastry and press in bottom and sides of tart pan. Trim edge. Place pan on ungreased baking sheet (see Tip, page 40).

Scatter shrimp and cream cheese in pie shell.

Combine remaining 5 ingredients in medium bowl. Pour over shrimp mixture. Bake on bottom rack in 375°F (190°C) oven for 50 to 55 minutes until knife inserted in centre comes out clean. Let stand on wire rack for 10 minutes before serving. Cuts into 6 wedges.

1 wedge: 663 Calories; 54.1 g Total Fat (8.6 g Mono, 1.3 g Poly, 27.0 g Sat); 454 mg Cholesterol; 23 g Carbohydrate; 0 g Fibre; 22 g Protein; 570 mg Sodium

Pictured on page 3 and below.

Left: Pepper And Ham Quiche, page 92
Right: Shrimp Quiche, page 92

Sweet caramelized onion, mild spinach and rich cheese raise canned salmon to an exceptional level. A beautiful and flavourful brunch dish.

make ahead

The tart may be baked 24 hours ahead of time, then covered and stored in the refrigerator overnight. To reheat, cover with foil and bake in a 400°F (205°C) oven for about 20 minutes or until heated through.

Spinach Salmon Tart

All-purpose flour	1 1/4 cups	300 mL
Cold butter (or hard margarine), cut up	1/3 cup	75 mL
Granulated sugar	1 tbsp.	15 mL
Dill weed	1/2 tsp.	2 mL
Salt	1/4 tsp.	1 mL
Egg yolks (large), fork-beaten	2	2
Ice water	3 tbsp.	50 mL
Butter (or hard margarine)	2 tbsp.	30 mL
Sliced onion	3 cups	750 mL
Dijon mustard	2 tbsp.	30 mL
Box of frozen chopped spinach, thawed and squeezed dry	10 oz.	300 g
Can of skinless, boneless pink salmon, drained and flaked	6 oz.	170 g
Large eggs	3	3
Sour cream	1/2 cup	125 mL
Grated Parmesan cheese	1/4 cup	60 mL
Lemon pepper	1/2 tsp.	2 mL
Grated havarti cheese	1/2 cup	125 mL

Process first 5 ingredients in food processor until mixture resembles coarse crumbs (see Note).

Add egg yolks and ice water. Pulse with on/off motion until mixture just starts to come together. Do not overprocess. Turn out onto lightly floured surface. Shape into slightly flattened disc. Wrap with plastic wrap. Chill for 30 minutes. Roll out pastry on lightly floured surface to fit ungreased 9 inch (22 cm) tart pan with fluted sides and removable bottom. Carefully lift pastry and press in bottom and up side of tart pan. Trim edge. Place pan on baking sheet (see Tip, page 40). Chill, covered, for 1 hour. Cover pastry with parchment paper, bringing paper up over edge. Fill halfway up side with dried beans. Bake on bottom rack in 375°F (190°C) oven for 15 minutes. Remove from oven. Carefully remove parchment paper and beans, reserving beans for next time you bake pastry. Bake crust for another 10 minutes until golden. Let stand on baking sheet on wire rack for 10 minutes.

Melt second amount of butter in large frying pan on medium. Add onion. Cook for about 15 minutes, stirring often, until caramelized. Remove from heat.

(continued on next page)

Spread mustard on bottom of crust. Scatter spinach and salmon overtop. Sprinkle caramelized onion on top.

Beat next 4 ingredients in medium bowl until frothy. Carefully pour over onion.

Sprinkle with havarti cheese. Bake in 375°F (190°C) oven for 35 to 40 minutes until cheese is golden. Let stand on wire rack for 10 minutes before serving. Cuts into 8 wedges.

1 wedge: 230 Calories; 23.8 g Total Fat (3.2 g Mono, 0.6 g Poly, 14.0 g Sat); 200 mg Cholesterol; 22 g Carbohydrate; 2 g Fibre; 15 g Protein; 500 mg Sodium

Pictured below.

Note: If you don't have a food processor, combine flour, sugar, dill weed and salt in a medium bowl. Cut in the butter until mixture resembles coarse crumbs. Stir in the egg yolk and water with a fork until mixture just starts to come together. Continue as directed.

This makes a fabulous and hearty dinner—perfect paired with a green salad.

Salmon Pie

Medium potatoes, quartered	5	5
Butter (or hard margarine)	2 tbsp.	30 mL
Chopped onion	1 cup	250 mL
Milk	2 tbsp.	30 mL
Fresh dill (or 1/2 tsp., 2 mL, dried)	2 tsp.	10 mL
Onion salt	1/2 tsp.	2 mL
Salt	1/2 tsp.	2 mL
Pepper	1/4 tsp.	1 mL
Cans of red salmon (7.5 oz., 213 g, each), drained, 1/3 cup (75 mL) liquid reserved, skin and round bones removed, flaked	2	2

Pastry for 2 crust 10 inch (22 cm) pie

SAUCE		
Butter (or hard margarine)	1/4 cup	60 mL
All-purpose flour	1/4 cup	60 mL
Paprika	1/4 tsp.	1 mL
Salt	1/8 tsp.	0.5 mL
Pepper	1/8 tsp.	0.5 mL
Milk	1 2/3 cups	400 mL
Reserved salmon liquid	1/3 cup	75 mL

Fresh dill, for garnish

Pour water into large saucepan until about 1 inch (2.5 cm) deep. Add potato. Cover. Bring to a boil. Reduce heat to medium. Boil gently for 12 to 15 minutes until tender. Drain. Set aside.

Melt butter in small frying pan on medium. Add onion. Cook for about 5 minutes, stirring occasionally until onion is soft. Add to potatoes. Stir.

Add next 5 ingredients to potato mixture. Mash. Mixture should be stiff.

Add salmon. Stir. Cool to room temperature.

Divide pastry into 2 portions, making 1 portion slightly larger than the other. Shape each portion into slightly flattened disc. Roll out larger portion on lightly floured surface to about 1/8 inch (3 mm) thickness. Line 10 inch (25 cm) pie plate. Spread salmon mixture in pie shell. Roll out smaller portion on lightly floured surface to about 1/8 inch (3 mm) thickness. Dampen edge of pastry

(continued on next page)

shell with water. Cover with remaining pastry. Trim and crimp decorative edge to seal. Cut several small vents in top to allow steam to escape. Bake in 400°F (205°C) oven for about 35 minutes until browned. Reduce heat to 350°F (175°C). Bake for about 40 minutes until pastry is golden brown (see Tip, page 42). Let stand on wire rack for 10 minutes before serving. Cuts into 6 wedges.

Sauce: Melt butter in small saucepan on medium. Add next 4 ingredients. Stir. Slowly add milk and reserved salmon liquid, stirring until smooth. Bring to a boil, stirring constantly, until thickened. Serve with Salmon Pie.

Sprinkle individual servings with dill. Serves 6.

1 wedge: 901 Calories; 41.4 g Total Fat (3.3 g Mono, 0.5 g Poly, 13.0 g Sat); 85 mg Cholesterol; 113 g Carbohydrate; 8 g Fibre; 34 g Protein; 877 mg Sodium

Pictured below and on back cover.

Left: Salmon Pie, page 96
Right: Curried Tuna Quiche, page 98

Fusilli pasta adds an attractive and unique touch to traditional quiche. To lighten your work, use a pre-grated mozzarella and Cheddar cheese blend.

Curried Tuna Quiche

Pastry for 9 inch (22 cm) pie shell

Cooked fusilli pasta (about 2/3 cup, 150 mL, uncooked)	1 cup	250 mL
Grated zucchini (with peel), squeezed dry	1 cup	250 mL
Can of flaked white tuna in water, drained	6 oz.	170 g
Grated medium Cheddar cheese	1/2 cup	125 mL
Grated mozzarella cheese	1/2 cup	125 mL
Large eggs	3	3
All-purpose flour	1 tbsp.	15 mL
Curry powder	1 tsp.	5 mL
Salt	1/2 tsp.	2 mL
Pepper	1/4 tsp.	1 mL
Skim evaporated milk	1 1/4 cups	300 mL
Roma (plum) tomatoes, sliced	2	2

Roll out pastry on lightly floured surface to 1/8 inch (3 mm) thickness. Line 9 inch (22 cm) pie plate. Trim, leaving 1/2 inch (12 mm) overhang. Roll under and crimp decorative edge.

Scatter next 5 ingredients in pie shell. Set aside.

Beat next 5 ingredients in medium bowl until smooth.

Add evaporated milk. Stir. Pour into pie shell.

Top with tomato. Bake on bottom rack in 350°F (175°C) oven for 60 to 65 minutes until knife inserted in centre comes out clean. Let stand for 10 minutes before serving. Cuts into 6 wedges.

1 wedge: 381 Calories; 16.4 g Total Fat (1.1 g Mono, 0.5 g Poly, 7.3 g Sat); 138 mg Cholesterol; 36 g Carbohydrate; 1 g Fibre; 21 g Protein; 668 mg Sodium

Pictured on page 97 and on back cover.

Onion And Potato Tart

Pastry for 2 crust 9 inch (22 cm) pie shell

Chopped peeled potatoes	2 3/4 cups	675 mL
Grated Gruyére cheese	1 1/4 cups	300 mL
Dried thyme	1/2 tsp.	2 mL
Butter (or hard margarine)	1 1/2 tbsp.	25 mL
Coarsely chopped onion	4 1/2 cups	1.1 L
Seasoned salt	1 tsp.	5 mL
Ground nutmeg	1/8 tsp.	0.5 mL
Pepper	1/8 tsp.	0.5 mL
Large eggs	5	5
Homogenized milk	1 1/2 cups	375 mL

This quiche is a very filling brunch dish with simple flavours that will please most palates.

Roll out pastry on lightly floured surface to about 1/8 inch (3 mm) thickness. Line 10 inch (25 cm) glass pie plate. Trim, leaving 1/2 inch (12 mm) overhang. Roll under and press against pie plate. Make decorative edge. Prick bottom and sides of pie shell with fork in several places. Place on ungreased baking sheet. Roll out scraps and make cut-outs with small cookie cutter. Place on same baking sheet. Cover pie shell with parchment paper, bringing paper up over edge. Fill halfway up side with dried beans. Bake in 375°F (190°C) oven for 15 minutes. Remove pie crust. Carefully remove parchment paper and beans, reserving beans for next time you bake pastry. Bake cut-outs for 2 to 3 minutes more until firm and starting to turn golden. Bake crust for another 10 minutes until golden.

Pour water into medium saucepan until about 1 inch (2.5 cm) deep. Add potato. Cover. Bring to a boil. Reduce heat to medium. Boil gently for 12 to 15 minutes until tender. Drain. Cool. Break up potatoes with fork or pastry blender until size of large peas. Scatter in bottom of crust.

Sprinkle with cheese and thyme.

Melt butter in large frying pan on medium. Add onion. Cook for about 15 minutes, stirring occasionally until soft. Reduce heat to low.

Sprinkle next 3 ingredients over onion. Cover. Cook for about 10 minutes, stirring occasionally until onion is browned. Spread over cheese.

Beat eggs and milk in small bowl until frothy. Carefully pour over onion mixture. Gently shake to allow spaces to fill in. Arrange cut-outs decoratively over tart. Bake on bottom rack in oven for 55 to 60 minutes until set and golden. Let stand on wire rack for 10 minutes before serving. Cuts into 8 wedges.

1 wedge: 505 Calories; 26.1 g Total Fat (2.7 g Mono, 0.5 g Poly, 12.5 g Sat); 175 mg Cholesterol; 54 g Carbohydrate; 3 g Fibre; 14 g Protein; 700 mg Sodium

Pictured on page 101.

A nutty oat crust holds vegetables, a curry-flavoured custard and our new favourite grain—quinoa (KEEN-wah). One bite and it's sure to be your favourite, too!

about quinoa

Known as the "mother grain" by the Incas who first cultivated this near-perfect seed, quinoa contains the highest amount of protein of any grain and all eight essential amino acids, making it a complete protein. If that weren't enough, it's also low in fat and carbohydrates and an overall excellent source of nutrients. It's been compared to couscous, and does have a texture and light flavour similar to that grain. Quinoa can be used as a substitute in many recipes in which you might use rice, couscous or even pasta.

Vegetable Quinoa Pie

NUT CRUST		
Quick-cooking rolled oats	1 1/2 cups	375 mL
All-purpose flour	1 cup	250 mL
Butter (or hard margarine), softened	1/2 cup	125 mL
Finely chopped unsalted mixed nuts, toasted (see Tip, page 9)	1/2 cup	125 mL
Brown sugar, packed	2 tbsp.	30 mL
VEGETABLE PIE		
Prepared vegetable broth	1 cup	250 mL
Salt	1/8 tsp.	0.5 mL
Quinoa, rinsed and drained	2/3 cup	150 mL
Cooking oil	2 tsp.	10 mL
Chopped fresh white mushrooms	3 cups	750 mL
Chopped onion	2 cups	500 mL
Garlic cloves, minced (or 1/2 tsp., 2 mL, powder)	2	2
Chopped cauliflower	3 cups	750 mL
Chopped red pepper	1 cup	250 mL
Grated carrot	1 cup	250 mL
All-purpose flour	2 tbsp.	30 mL
Curry powder	2 tsp.	10 mL
Salt	1/2 tsp.	2 mL
Pepper	1/4 tsp.	1 mL
Grated Gruyère cheese	1 cup	250 mL
Grated sharp Cheddar cheese	1 cup	250 mL
Large eggs	6	6
Milk	2 cups	500 mL

Nut Crust: Mix all 5 ingredients in medium bowl until mixture resembles coarse crumbs. Press firmly in bottom and halfway up sides of greased 3 quart (3 L) shallow baking dish. Bake in 350°F (175°C) oven for about 15 minutes until just golden. Let stand on wire rack to cool.

Vegetable Pie: Combine broth and salt in small saucepan. Bring to a boil. Add quinoa. Stir. Reduce heat to medium-low. Simmer, covered, for about 20 minutes, without stirring, until quinoa is tender and liquid is absorbed. Fluff with fork. Transfer to large bowl.

(continued on next page)

Heat cooking oil in large frying pan on medium. Add next 3 ingredients. Cook for about 10 minutes, stirring often, until onion is softened.

Add next 3 ingredients. Stir. Sprinkle with next 4 ingredients. Heat and stir for 1 minute. Add to quinoa. Stir. Let stand for 10 minutes.

Add Gruyère and Cheddar cheese. Stir.

Whisk eggs and milk in medium bowl until combined. Add to quinoa mixture. Stir. Pour into crust. Spread over crust. Bake for about 1 hour until knife inserted in centre comes out clean and top is golden. Let stand on wire rack for 10 minutes before serving. Cuts into 6 pieces.

1 wedge: 790 Calories; 43.9 g Total Fat (13.0 g Mono, 3.5 g Poly, 20.3 g Sat); 300 mg Cholesterol; 71 g Carbohydrate; 8 g Fibre; 32 g Protein; 752 mg Sodium

Pictured below.

Left: Onion And Potato Tart, page 99
Right: Vegetable Quinoa Pie, page 100

An attractive, light quiche. Creamy feta gives a unique flavour.

about feta

Feta is a soft, sometimes creamy cheese that is white, rindless and crumbly. It usually has a sharp, salty taste and is sometimes known as pickled cheese because it is stored and sold in brine. It's traditionally made with sheep and goat's milk, and despite the fact that it's best known by an Italian name (*feta* is from the Italian word *fetta*, meaning "slice"), it is the national cheese of Greece.

Leek And Tomato Quiche

Medium leeks (white part only)	2	2
Olive (or cooking) oil	2 tsp.	10 mL
Pastry for 9 inch (22 cm) deep dish pie shell		
Crumbled feta cheese (about 3 oz., 85 g)	2/3 cup	150 mL
Large eggs	6	6
Half-and-half cream (or homogenized milk)	1 3/4 cups	425 mL
Honey Dijon mustard	2 tbsp.	30 mL
Salt	1/4 tsp.	1 mL
Pepper	1/4 tsp.	1 mL
Large roma (plum) tomato, cut into 6 slices	1	1

Cut leeks lengthwise into thirds. Brush with olive oil. Preheat electric grill for 5 minutes or gas barbecue to medium-high. Cook leeks, cut-side down, on greased grill for about 5 minutes until softened and grill marks appear. Remove from heat. Cool.

Roll out pastry on lightly floured surface to about 1/8 inch (3 mm) thickness. Line 9 inch (22 cm) deep dish pie plate. Trim, leaving 1/2 inch (12 mm) overhang. Roll under and crimp decorative edge.

Scatter feta cheese over bottom of pie shell. Arrange leeks in spoke pattern over cheese.

Whisk next 5 ingredients in medium bowl until well combined. Carefully pour over leeks.

Place tomato slices between leeks, near edge of crust. Bake on bottom rack in 375°F (190°C) oven for about 50 minutes until knife inserted in centre comes out clean. Let stand on wire rack for 10 minutes before serving. Cuts into 6 wedges.

1 wedge: 362 Calories; 26.3 g Total Fat (4.2 g Mono, 0.6 g Poly, 12.1 g Sat); 266 mg Cholesterol; 20 g Carbohydrate; trace Fibre; 12 g Protein; 516 mg Sodium

Pictured on page 105.

Tomato Basil Pie

Butter (or hard margarine)	1 tbsp.	15 mL
Chopped green pepper	1 cup	250 mL
Chopped onion	1 cup	250 mL
Unbaked 9 inch (22 cm) pie shell	1	1
Large eggs	3	3
Mayonnaise	1/2 cup	125 mL
All-purpose flour	1 tbsp.	15 mL
Salt	1/2 tsp.	2 mL
Pepper	1/2 tsp.	2 mL
Fine dry bread crumbs	1/2 cup	125 mL
Finely shredded basil	3 tbsp.	50 mL
Medium tomatoes, cut into 1/4 inch (6 mm) slices	2	2
Swiss (or Monterey Jack) cheese, sliced and cut into wide strips	4 oz.	113 g

Melt butter in medium frying pan on medium-high. Add green pepper and onion. Cook for 5 to 10 minutes, stirring often, until onion is softened. Remove from heat. Cool slightly. Spread in pie shell.

Whisk next 5 ingredients in medium bowl until smooth. Carefully pour over onion mixture.

Sprinkle with bread crumbs and basil. Bake on bottom rack in 350°F (175°C) oven for about 30 minutes until starting to set. Remove from oven.

Layer tomato slices alternately with cheese strips, slightly overlapping, on top of pie. Bake for another 25 minutes until pastry is golden and cheese is melted. Let stand on wire rack for 10 minutes before serving. Cuts into 6 wedges.

1 wedge: 488 Calories; 34.2 g Total Fat (0.5 g Mono, 0.1 g Poly, 11.3 g Sat); 143 mg Cholesterol; 32 g Carbohydrate; 2 g Fibre; 12 g Protein; 623 mg Sodium

Pictured on page 105.

Firm-textured quiche accented with nutty Swiss cheese, fresh tomato and basil. Wonderful for a summer potluck.

about storing basil

Fresh basil is a highly perishable herb that doesn't keep long, even when refrigerated. Use it as soon as you can after purchasing it. If you need to store it, wrap it in slightly damp paper towels and keep it in the fridge to keep it fresher longer, and don't wash it until just before you need to use it. To preserve it for longer, you can mix fresh leaves with olive oil and puree them into a paste in a blender or food processor. You can also freeze basil whole or chopped, either in a resealable freezer bag (if whole) or covered with water in an ice cube tray (if chopped).

Use your favourite blue cheese in this rich brunch or luncheon pie. Try Stilton, Roquefort or Gorgonzola.

about blue cheese

For some people, the sight of blue cheese is a bit of a turn-off. Aren't you supposed to throw out moldy cheese, not eat it? In most cases that is true, but in the case of blue cheese, whose molds are *Penicillium*, the mold is the point! These cheeses get their blue colour from the interaction of the molds with the air, and they're perfectly safe to eat. They are very strong tasting and smelling, however, so if you're not sure, try starting with a mild variety, such as Cambozola or Bleu de Bresse.

Blue Onion Pie

Large eggs	3	3
Ricotta cheese	1 cup	250 mL
Homogenized milk	3/4 cup	175 mL
Sliced green onion	1/2 cup	125 mL
Chopped fresh parsley (or 1 1/2 tsp., 7 mL, flakes)	2 tbsp.	30 mL
Salt	1/2 tsp.	2 mL
Coarsely ground pepper, sprinkle		
Unbaked 9 inch (22 cm) pie shell	1	1
Blue cheese (such as Danish Blue), broken up	4 oz.	113 g

Whisk eggs in medium bowl until frothy. Add next 6 ingredients. Stir well. Pour into pie shell.

Sprinkle blue cheese over egg mixture. Bake on bottom rack in 350°F (175°C) oven for about 50 minutes until golden. Let stand on wire rack for 10 minutes before serving. Cuts into 6 wedges.

1 wedge: 349 Calories; 22.7 g Total Fat (1.8 g Mono, 0.2 g Poly, 11.9 g Sat); 149 mg Cholesterol; 20 g Carbohydrate; trace Fibre; 15 g Protein; 706 mg Sodium

Pictured at right.

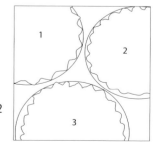

1. Leek And Tomato Quiche, page 102
2. Blue Onion Pie, above
3. Tomato Basil Pie, page 103

A great, gooey, runny filling. These freeze well.

variation

Nutty Butter Tarts: Divide 1/2 cup chopped walnuts or pecans in tart shells with raisins.

Butter Tarts *A Classic!*

Raisins, coarsely chopped (or currants)	1/3 cup	75 mL
Unbaked tart shells	12	12
Large egg	1	1
Brown sugar, packed	1/2 cup	125 mL
Corn syrup	1/4 cup	60 mL
Butter (or hard margarine), softened	3 tbsp.	50 mL
White vinegar	1 1/2 tsp.	7 mL
Vanilla extract	1/4 tsp.	1 mL
Salt	1/8 tsp.	0.5 mL

Divide raisins evenly among tart shells.

Beat egg with fork in medium bowl until frothy. Add next 6 ingredients. Stir well. Spoon over raisins until 3/4 full. Bake on bottom rack in 375°F (190°C) oven for about 15 minutes until pastry is golden brown and filling rises up to form a dome. Remove tarts from baking sheet to wire rack to cool. Makes 12 tarts.

1 tart: 180 Calories; 8.1 g Total Fat (0.7 g Mono, 0.1 g Poly, 4.0 g Sat); 29 mg Cholesterol; 26 g Carbohydrate; trace Fibre; 1.3 g Protein; 133 mg Sodium

Pictured at right.

These sweet tarts have a surprise cherry filling hidden beneath a silky lemon custard. Even with a whipped cream topping, they freeze beautifully. For added sparkle, dust with a sprinkle of golden sanding sugar just before serving.

Lemon Cherry Tartlets

Frozen mini tart shells, thawed	36	36
Cherry jam, fruit finely chopped	6 tbsp.	100 mL
Large eggs	3	3
Granulated sugar	1 cup	250 mL
Butter (or hard margarine), cut up	1/4 cup	60 mL
Lemon juice	1/4 cup	60 mL
Grated lemon zest	1 tsp.	5 mL
Whipping cream	1 cup	250 mL
Instant vanilla pudding powder	1 tbsp.	15 mL

(continued on next page)

Arrange tart shells on 2 baking sheets with sides. Bake on separate racks in 375°F (190°C) oven for 10 to 12 minutes, switching position of baking sheets at halftime, until golden.

Spoon 1/2 tsp. (2 mL) jam in each shell. Set aside.

Beat eggs and sugar in medium bowl until thick and pale. Transfer to medium saucepan.

Add next 3 ingredients. Heat and stir on medium for about 10 minutes until thickened and just starting to boil. Transfer to 4 cup (1 L) heatproof liquid measure. Pour evenly into tart shells. Chill for about 1 hour until set.

Beat whipping cream and pudding powder in separate medium bowl for about 5 minutes until stiff peaks form. Spoon into piping bag fitted with large star tip. Pipe over egg mixture in tarts. Chill until set. Makes 36 tartlets.

1 tartlet: 144 Calories; 8.7 g Total Fat (3.3 g Mono, 0.7 g Poly, 4.0 g Sat); 30 mg Cholesterol; 16 g Carbohydrate; trace Fibre; 1 g Protein; 112 mg Sodium

Pictured below.

make ahead

The tartlets may be stored (with the piped whipped cream on top) in a single layer in an airtight container in the freezer for up to one month. Thaw them at room temperature for about one hour before serving.

Top: Butter Tarts, page 106
Bottom: Lemon Cherry Tartlets, page 106

Caramel-coated pecans and a drizzle of chocolate top a rich cheesecake filling. An elegant presentation for when the "wow" factor counts.

Praline Cheesecake Tarts

Unbaked tart shells	24	24
CHEESECAKE FILLING		
Cream cheese, softened	8 oz.	250 g
Sour cream	1 cup	250 mL
Granulated sugar	3/4 cup	175 mL
All-purpose flour	2 tbsp.	30 mL
Large eggs	2	2
Vanilla extract	1 tsp.	5 mL
PRALINE		
Caramel (or butterscotch) ice cream topping	1/2 cup	125 mL
Finely chopped pecans, toasted (see Tip, page 9)	1/2 cup	125 mL
Semi-sweet chocolate chips	1/2 cup	125 mL
Butter (or hard margarine)	2 tbsp.	30 mL

Arrange tart shells on 2 baking sheets with sides. Bake in 350°F (175°C) oven for 10 to 12 minutes until golden. Cool.

Cheesecake Filling: Beat first 4 ingredients in large bowl until smooth. Add eggs, 1 at a time, beating after each addition until just combined. Add vanilla. Stir. Spoon about 2 1/2 tbsp. (37 mL) in each tart shell. Bake for about 20 minutes until set. Remove tarts from baking sheet to wire rack to cool.

Praline: Combine ice cream topping and pecans in small bowl. Makes about 2/3 cup (150 mL). Spoon about 1 tsp. over each tart filling.

Heat and stir chocolate chips and butter in small saucepan on lowest heat until almost melted. Remove from heat. Stir until smooth. Spoon into pastry bag fitted with small writing tip or small resealable freezer bag with tiny piece snipped off corner. Drizzle chocolate in decorative pattern over praline on each tart. Makes 24 tarts.

1 tart: 229 Calories; 14 g Total Fat (1.6 g Mono, 0.6 g Poly, 7.0 g Sat); 40 mg Cholesterol; 24 g Carbohydrate; 1 g Fibre; 3 g Protein; 142 mg Sodium

Pictured at right.

These tantalizing summer treats make the perfect barbecue or picnic dessert. Best served the day they are made— an easy recipe to double.

Strawberry Cheese Tarts

Unbaked tart shells	12	12
Semi-sweet chocolate chips	1/3 cup	75 mL
Butter (or hard margarine)	1 tbsp.	15 mL
Cream cheese, softened	4 oz.	125 g
Granulated sugar	1/2 cup	125 mL
Sour cream	3 tbsp.	50 mL
Orange extract	1/4 tsp.	1 mL
Vanilla extract	1/4 tsp.	1 mL
STRAWBERRY TOPPING		
Sliced fresh strawberries	1 cup	250 mL
Strawberry (or other red) jelly, melted	2 tbsp.	30 mL

Arrange tart shells on baking sheet with sides. Bake in 375°F (190°C) oven for 10 to 12 minutes until golden. Cool.

Heat and stir chocolate chips and butter in small saucepan on low until almost melted. Remove from heat. Stir until smooth. Spoon evenly into bottom of tart shells. Chill until set.

Beat next 5 ingredients in small bowl for about 5 minutes until smooth. Spread over chocolate. Chill for 1 hour.

Strawberry Topping: Toss strawberries and jelly in small bowl until coated. Spoon over cream cheese mixture. Chill until set. Makes 12 tarts.

1 tart: 200 Calories; 11.1 g Total Fat (0.7 g Mono, 0.1 g Poly, 6.2 g Sat); 18 mg Cholesterol; 24 g Carbohydrate; 1 g Fibre; 2 g Protein; 110 mg Sodium

Pictured on page 3 and at right.

Keep a supply of these creamy berry tarts in your freezer for a quick treat when company drops by.

Frozen Yogurt Tarts

Frozen mini tart shells, thawed	24	24
Cream cheese, softened	4 oz.	125 g
Container of blueberry yogurt	6 oz.	175 g
Blueberry jam	1/2 cup	125 mL

Arrange tart shells on baking sheet with sides. Bake in 375°F (190°C) oven for 10 to 12 minutes until golden. Cool.

(continued on next page)

Beat cream cheese in small bowl until smooth. Add yogurt and jam. Beat well. Divide among tart shells. Freeze. Makes 24 tarts.

1 tart: 40 Calories; 1.6 g Total Fat (0 g Mono, 0 g Poly, 1.1 g Sat); 5 mg Cholesterol; 6 g Carbohydrate; 0 g Fibre; 1 g Protein; 20 mg Sodium

Pictured on page 3 and below.

Top: Strawberry Cheese Tarts, page 110
Bottom: Frozen Yogurt Tarts, page 110

A sweet, smooth, egg custard in a light, flaky pastry. Enjoy warm or at room temperature.

tip

Reheat tarts on ungreased baking sheet in 250°F (120°C) oven for about 5 minutes.

Rich Egg Custard Tarts

TART PASTRY

All-purpose flour	2 cups	500 mL
Cold lard, cut into 4 pieces	1/2 cup	125 mL
Cold butter (or hard margarine)	1/4 cup	60 mL
Egg yolk (large), fork-beaten	1	1
Ice water	1/4 cup	60 mL

CUSTARD

Granulated sugar	1/2 cup	125 mL
Custard powder	1 tbsp.	15 mL
Water	2/3 cup	150 mL
Half-and-half cream	1/3 cup	75 mL
Drop of yellow food colouring (optional)	1	1
Large eggs	4	4

Tart Pastry: Process first 3 ingredients in food processor until mixture resembles coarse crumbs. Add egg yolk and water. Process with on/off motion until mixture starts to come together. Do not overprocess. Turn out onto lightly floured surface. Shape pastry into slightly flattened disc. Wrap with plastic wrap. Chill for 1 hour. Roll out pastry on lightly floured surface to 1/4 inch (6 mm) thickness. Cut into 3 1/2 inch (9 cm) circles with floured cutter. Line tart or muffin pan with circles.

Custard: Combine sugar and custard powder in small saucepan. Slowly add water, stirring until smooth. Heat and stir on medium until mixture comes to a boil and sugar is dissolved. Pour into small bowl. Cover with plastic wrap directly on surface to prevent skin from forming. Chill until cool. Stir in cream and food colouring.

Beat first egg with fork in small cup. Stir into custard mixture. Repeat with remaining eggs, stirring in each beaten egg 1 at a time. Fill tart shells to within 1/4 inch (6 mm) of top. Bake on bottom rack in 300°F (150°C) oven for about 45 minutes until knife inserted in centre comes out clean and custard is set. Let stand in pan for 10 minutes before removing to wire rack to cool. Makes 12 tarts.

1 tart: 250 Calories; 15.0 g Total Fat (5.2 g Mono, 1.2 g Poly, 6.9 g Sat); 109 mg Cholesterol; 25 g Carbohydrate; trace Fibre; 5 g Protein; 59 mg Sodium

Pictured on page 115.

Pumpkin Tartlets

Warmly spiced pumpkin pie tartlets with a rich, creamy texture. A heavenly aroma will fill your house while these treats are in the oven.

PASTRY

All-purpose flour	2 cups	500 mL
Brown sugar, packed	1 tbsp.	15 mL
Salt	1/2 tsp.	2 mL
Cold butter (or hard margarine), cut up	1 cup	250 mL
Water	1/3 cup	75 mL

FILLING

Large eggs	2	2
All-purpose flour	2 tbsp.	30 mL
Ground cinnamon	3/4 tsp.	4 mL
Ground ginger	1/2 tsp.	2 mL
Ground allspice	1/4 tsp.	1 mL
Ground nutmeg	1/4 tsp.	1 mL
Salt	1/4 tsp.	1 mL
Can of pure pumpkin (without spices)	14 oz.	398 mL
Can of sweetened condensed milk	11 oz.	300 mL

Whipped cream (or frozen whipped topping, thawed), for garnish

Pastry: Combine first 3 ingredients in large bowl. Cut in butter until mixture resembles coarse crumbs.

Drizzle water over flour mixture, stirring with fork until mixture starts to come together. Do not overmix. Turn out pastry onto work surface. Shape into slightly flattened disc. Roll out on lightly floured surface to 1/8 inch (3 mm) thickness. Cut into 2 1/2 inch (6.4 cm) circles with floured cutter. Line tartlet pans or mini muffin cups with circles.

Filling: Whisk eggs in medium bowl until frothy. Add next 6 ingredients. Whisk to combine.

Add pumpkin and condensed milk. Stir until smooth. Spoon about 1 1/2 tbsp. (25 mL) filling in each pastry shell. Bake on bottom rack in 375°F (190°C) oven for about 20 minutes until wooden pick inserted in centre comes out clean. Let stand in pan for 10 minutes before removing to wire rack to cool.

Garnish with whipped cream. Makes 36 tartlets.

1 tartlet: 107 Calories; 6.0 g Total Fat (1.3 g Mono, 0.2 g Poly, 3.8 g Sat); 28 mg Cholesterol; 12 g Carbohydrate; trace Fibre; 2 g Protein; 99 mg Sodium

Pictured on page 115.

A rich, red tomato filling in golden pastry cups, topped with lightly browned goat cheese. Tartlets may be frozen after baking and reheated later for a perfect pre-made appetizer.

about goat cheese

Delicious and versatile goat cheese, also known as chèvre, is usually made from 100% goat's milk. It starts off soft and creamy and hardens as it ages, acquiring a sharper taste along the way. If the goat cheese you buy has "pur chèvre" on the label, that means the cheese was made solely from goat's milk. If the label says "mi-chèvre," it was made with half goat and half cow's milk. All goat cheese has a tart flavour, but if yours tastes sour, it may mean it has gone bad. Avoid storing it for longer than two weeks in your refrigerator.

Tomato Goat Cheese Tartlets

Olive (or cooking) oil	2 tsp.	10 mL
Chopped onion	1 cup	250 mL
Can of diced tomatoes, drained	14 oz.	398 mL
Granulated sugar	1/2 tsp.	2 mL
Pepper	1/8 tsp.	0.5 mL
Chopped fresh parsley (or 1 1/4 tsp., 6 mL, flakes)	1 1/2 tbsp.	25 mL
Chopped fresh basil (or 3/4 tsp., 4 mL, dried)	1 tbsp.	15 mL
Large eggs, fork-beaten	2	2
Frozen mini tart shells, thawed	24	24
Goat (chèvre) cheese (about 1/3 cup, 75 mL), cut up	2 oz.	57 g

Heat olive oil in medium frying pan on medium. Add onion. Cook for about 8 minutes, stirring often, until soft and golden. Increase heat to medium-high.

Add next 3 ingredients. Cook for about 2 minutes, stirring occasionally, until liquid is evaporated. Remove from heat. Add parsley and basil. Stir. Let stand for 15 minutes.

Add eggs. Stir well.

Arrange tart shells on baking sheet with sides. Spoon about 1 tbsp. (15 mL) filling in each shell.

Place about 1/2 tsp. (2 mL) goat cheese over filling in each shell. Bake on bottom rack in 375°F (190°C) oven for 20 to 25 minutes until filling is set and crust is golden. Let stand in pan for 10 minutes before serving. Makes 24 tartlets.

1 tartlet: 95 Calories; 5.9 g Total Fat (2.6 g Mono, 0.6 g Poly, 2.0 g Sat); 19 mg Cholesterol; 8 g Carbohydrate; trace Fibre; 2 g Protein; 145 mg Sodium

Pictured at right.

1. Rich Egg Custard Tarts, page 112
2. Tomato Goat Cheese Tartlets, above
3. Pumpkin Tartlets, page 113

The sweet taste of sautéed onions is a nice complement to the Brie cheese.

brie versus camembert

You may have seen both of these cheeses at the grocery store or cheese shop and noticed that they look quite similar to each other. Perhaps you have wondered, what's the difference? The answer is, not very much. Both cheeses are surface-ripened only, and have edible rinds with a slightly mushroomy flavour. Both are mild-tasting, have soft, yellowish insides and get a little runny if left for a while at room temperature. Brie is named for an area outside of Paris; Camembert is named after the French village where it has been made for centuries.

Onion And Brie Tartlets

Olive (or cooking) oil	2 tsp.	10 mL
Finely chopped onion	2/3 cup	150 mL
Granulated sugar	2 tsp.	10 mL
Red wine vinegar	2 tsp.	10 mL
Large eggs	2	2
Brie cheese, chopped	4 oz.	113 g
Half-and-half cream	1/3 cup	75 mL
Ground nutmeg	1/2 tsp.	2 mL
Frozen mini tart shells, thawed	24	24

Heat olive oil in small frying pan on medium-low. Add onion. Cook for about 10 minutes, stirring occasionally, until soft.

Add sugar and vinegar. Heat and stir until sugar is dissolved. Remove from heat.

Process next 4 ingredients in blender until smooth.

Arrange tart shells on baking sheet with sides. Divide onion mixture evenly in shells. Spoon cream mixture in shells until about 3/4 full. Bake on bottom rack in 375°F (190°C) oven for about 25 minutes until set. Let stand in pan for 10 minutes before serving. Makes 24 tartlets.

1 tartlet: 106 Calories; 7.1 g Total Fat (3.0 g Mono, 0.7 g Poly, 2.8 g Sat); 24 mg Cholesterol; 8 g Carbohydrate; trace Fibre; 2 g Protein; 128 mg Sodium

Pictured below.

Date And Blue Cheese Tarts

Pastry for 2 crust 9 inch (22 cm) pie

Large eggs	2	2
Buttermilk (or soured milk, see Tip)	1/3 cup	75 mL
Ground nutmeg	1/2 tsp.	2 mL
Finely chopped pitted dates	1/2 cup	125 mL
Blue cheese, crumbled	1 1/2 oz.	43 g

Roll out pastry on lightly floured surface to 1/4 inch (6 mm) thickness. Cut into 3 1/4 inch (8.2 cm) circles with fluted cutter. Line tartlet pans or mini muffin cups with circles.

Whisk next 3 ingredients in medium bowl. Add dates and blue cheese. Stir well. Spoon about 2 tsp. (10 mL) date mixture in each shell. Bake on bottom rack in 375°F (190°C) oven for about 15 minutes until set. Let stand in pan for 10 minutes before serving. Makes 24 tarts.

1 tartlet: 104 Calories; 5.6 g Total Fat (0.2 g Mono, trace Poly, 2.5 g Sat); 23 mg Cholesterol; 12 g Carbohydrate; trace Fibre; 2 g Protein; 100 mg Sodium

Pictured below.

The savoury taste of blue cheese and the sweetness of dates are a perfect appetizer combination. These are super-quick and easy to make ahead of time. Serve warm or cold.

souring milk

To make soured milk, measure 1 tsp. (5 mL) white vinegar or lemon juice into a 1 cup (250 mL) liquid measure. Add enough milk to make 1/3 cup (75 mL). Stir. Let stand for 5 minutes.

Which came first, the chicken or the egg? In this recipe they come together. Pesto and cheese make this tasty mini quiche hard to beat.

about pesto

Pesto is an uncooked sauce originating in Genoa, Italy. It's traditionally made by pureeing or mashing together fresh basil, garlic, pine nuts and olive oil. Parmesan cheese can also be added, but it's not strictly a traditional ingredient. At one time, pestos were made only with basil, but these days, a variety of fresh herbs are used, including mint, lemon balm and even cilantro.

If you are a curry lover, add more of this distinctive spice to suit your taste. It makes lots, so you can keep extras in the freezer.

Pesto Chicken Tarts

Large eggs	4	4
Milk	1/2 cup	125 mL
Basil pesto	1/4 cup	60 mL
Grated Parmesan cheese	1/4 cup	60 mL
Pepper	1/4 tsp.	1 mL
Finely chopped cooked chicken (see Tip, page 81)	1 cup	250 mL
Unbaked tart shells	16	16
Grated Parmesan cheese	4 tsp.	20 mL

Beat first 5 ingredients in medium bowl until frothy. Add chicken. Stir.

Place tart shells on ungreased baking sheet with sides. Spoon about 2 tbsp. (30 mL) egg mixture into each tart shell. Sprinkle tarts with second amount of cheese. Bake on bottom rack in 375°F (190°C) oven for about 25 minutes until pastry is golden and wooden pick inserted in centre comes out clean. Let stand in pan for 10 minutes before serving. Makes 16 tarts.

1 tart: 152 Calories; 9.5 g Total Fat (0.3 g Mono, 0.2 g Poly, 3.5 g Sat); 69 mg Cholesterol; 10 g Carbohydrate; trace Fibre; 6 g Protein; 174 mg Sodium

Pictured at right.

Curried Beef Tarts

Lean ground beef	1 lb.	454 g
Medium onion, chopped	1	1
All-purpose flour	1 tbsp.	15 mL
Curry powder	2 tsp.	10 mL
Water	1/3 cup	75 mL
Large eggs, fork-beaten	3	3
Finely crumbled feta cheese	1 cup	250 mL
White vinegar	1 tbsp.	15 mL
Salt	3/4 tsp.	4 mL
Pepper	1/4 tsp.	1 mL
Unbaked tart shells	36	36

(continued on next page)

Scramble-fry ground beef and onion in large frying pan on medium-high for about 5 minutes until beef is no longer pink. Drain.

Reduce heat to medium. Sprinkle flour and curry powder over beef mixture. Heat and stir for 1 minute. Add water. Bring to a boil, stirring constantly, until thickened. Remove from heat. Cool.

Add next 5 ingredients. Stir well.

Arrange tart shells on 2 baking sheets with sides. Spoon about 1 1/2 tbsp. beef mixture in each tart shell. Bake on separate racks in 350°F (175°C) oven for 30 to 35 minutes, switching position of baking sheets at halftime, until golden. Let stand for 10 minutes before serving. Makes 36 tarts.

1 tart: 119 Calories; 6.8 g Total Fat (0.4 g Mono, 0.1 g Poly, 3.1 g Sat); 32 mg Cholesterol; 10 g Carbohydrate; trace Fibre; 4 g Protein; 176 mg Sodium

Pictured below.

Left: Pesto Chicken Tarts, page 118
Right: Curried Beef Tarts, page 118

Whether in a pie shell or tart shells, mushrooms and onions are always a welcome flavour combo.

Mushroom Quiche Tarts

Can of mushroom stems and pieces, drained	10 oz.	284 mL
Grated Swiss cheese (about 4 oz., 113 g)	1 cup	250 mL
Grated medium Cheddar cheese (about 2 oz., 57 g)	1/2 cup	125 mL
All-purpose flour	1/4 cup	60 mL
Salt	1/2 tsp.	2 mL
Pepper	1/4 tsp.	1 mL
Unbaked tart shells	16	16
Large eggs	4	4
Half-and-half cream (or homogenized milk)	1 cup	250 mL
Finely chopped green onions	1/4 cup	60 mL
Worcestershire sauce	1 tsp.	5 mL
Cayenne pepper	1/8 tsp.	0.5 mL

Toss first 6 ingredients together in medium bowl.

Scatter in bottom of tart shells.

Beat eggs until frothy. Add next 4 ingredients. Stir well. Spoon about 1 1/2 tbsp. (25 mL) over mushroom filling in each tart shell. Bake on bottom rack in 350°F (175°C) oven for about 55 minutes until set and golden. Let stand in pan for 10 minutes before serving. Makes 16 tarts.

1 tart: 174 Calories; 11.0 g Total Fat (0.8 g Mono, 0.1 g Poly, 5.6 g Sat); 73 mg Cholesterol; 13 g Carbohydrate; trace Fibre; 6 g Protein; 281 mg Sodium

Pictured at right.

A delicious little tart that will kick-start your taste buds.

tip

Wear gloves when chopping jalapeño peppers, and avoid touching your eyes.

Ricotta And Jalapeño Tarts

Cooking oil	2 tsp.	10 mL
Diced jalapeño pepper (see Tip)	2 tbsp.	30 mL
Grated carrot	2 tbsp.	30 mL
Sliced green onion	2 tbsp.	30 mL
Large egg	1	1
Ricotta cheese	1 cup	250 mL
Salt	1/2 tsp.	2 mL
Dried oregano	1/4 tsp.	1 mL
Frozen mini tart shells, thawed	20	20

(continued on next page)

Heat cooking oil in small frying pan on medium. Add next 3 ingredients. Cook for 2 to 3 minutes, stirring often, until soft. Remove from heat. Cool.

Whisk next 4 ingredients in small bowl. Add onion mixture. Stir well.

Arrange tart shells on baking sheet with sides. Spoon about 2 tsp. (10 mL) in each tart shell. Bake on bottom rack in 400°F (205°C) oven for 12 to 15 minutes until pastry is golden and filling is set. Let stand for 10 minutes before serving. Makes 20 tarts.

1 tartlet: 101 Calories; 6.8 g Total Fat (2.5 g Mono, 0.7 g Poly, 2.5 g Sat); 16 mg Cholesterol; 7 g Carbohydrate; trace Fibre; 3 g Protein; 174 mg Sodium

Pictured below.

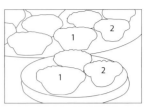

1. Mushroom Quiche Tarts, page 120
2. Ricotta And Jalapeño Tarts, page 120

Hot party appetizers are the first to need refilling. These freeze well—reheat in 325°F (160°C) oven for 15 to 20 minutes if thawed, or 30 to 40 minutes if still frozen.

Shrimp Tartlets

CREAM CHEESE PASTRY

Butter (or hard margarine), softened	1/2 cup	125 mL
Cream cheese, softened	4 oz.	125 g
All-purpose flour	1 cup	250 mL

SHRIMP FILLING

Chopped cooked shrimp	3/4 cup	175 mL
Large egg	1	1
Grated Swiss cheese	1 cup	250 mL
Milk	1/2 cup	125 mL
Chopped chives	1 tbsp.	15 mL
Dill weed	1/4 tsp.	1 mL
Onion powder	1/4 tsp.	1 mL
Salt	1/4 tsp.	1 mL
Pepper, just a pinch		

Cream Cheese Pastry: Beat butter and cream cheese in medium bowl until smooth. Stir in flour until soft dough forms. Divide into 24 equal balls. Press in bottom and up sides of tartlet pans or mini muffin cups.

Shrimp Filling: Divide shrimp evenly among tart shells.

Process remaining 8 ingredients in blender until smooth. Pour over shrimp in each tart shell until 3/4 full. Bake on bottom rack in 350°F (175°C) oven for 20 to 25 minutes until set. Let stand for 10 minutes before serving. Makes 24 tartlets.

1 tartlet: 97 Calories; 7.0 g Total Fat (1.0 g Mono, 0.2 g Poly, 4.5 g Sat); 42 mg Cholesterol; 4 g Carbohydrate; trace Fibre; 4 g Protein; 98 mg Sodium

Pictured at right.

Throughout this book measurements are given in Conventional and Metric measure. To compensate for differences between the two measurements due to rounding, a full metric measure is not always used. The cup used is the standard 8 fluid ounce. Temperature is given in degrees Fahrenheit and Celsius. Baking pan measurements are in inches and centimetres as well as quarts and litres. An exact metric conversion is given on this page as well as the working equivalent (Metric Standard Measure).

Pans

Conventional – Inches	Metric – Centimetres
8 × 8 inch	20 × 20 cm
9 × 9 inch	22 × 22 cm
9 × 13 inch	22 × 33 cm
10 × 15 inch	25 × 38 cm
11 × 17 inch	28 × 43 cm
8 × 2 inch round	20 × 5 cm
9 × 2 inch round	22 × 5 cm
10 × 4 1/2 inch tube	25 × 11 cm
8 × 4 × 3 inch loaf	20 × 10 × 7.5 cm
9 × 5 × 3 inch loaf	22 × 12.5 × 7.5 cm

Oven Temperatures

Fahrenheit (°F)	Celsius (°C)	Fahrenheit (°F)	Celsius (°C)
175°	80°	350°	175°
200°	95°	375°	190°
225°	110°	400°	205°
250°	120°	425°	220°
275°	140°	450°	230°
300°	150°	475°	240°
325°	160°	500°	260°

Spoons

Conventional Measure	Metric Exact Conversion Millilitre (mL)	Metric Standard Measure Millilitre (mL)
1/8 teaspoon (tsp.)	0.6 mL	0.5 mL
1/4 teaspoon (tsp.)	1.2 mL	1 mL
1/2 teaspoon (tsp.)	2.4 mL	2 mL
1 teaspoon (tsp.)	4.7 mL	5 mL
2 teaspoons (tsp.)	9.4 mL	10 mL
1 tablespoon (tbsp.)	14.2 mL	15 mL

Cups

1/4 cup (4 tbsp.)	56.8 mL	60 mL
1/3 cup (5 1/3 tbsp.)	75.6 mL	75 mL
1/2 cup (8 tbsp.)	113.7 mL	125 mL
2/3 cup (10 2/3 tbsp.)	151.2 mL	150 mL
3/4 cup (12 tbsp.)	170.5 mL	175 mL
1 cup (16 tbsp.)	227.3 mL	250 mL
4 1/2 cups	1022.9 mL	1000 mL(1 L)

Dry Measurements

Conventional Measure Ounces (oz.)	Metric Exact Conversion Grams (g)	Metric Standard Measure Grams (g)
1 oz.	28.3 g	28 g
2 oz.	56.7 g	57 g
3 oz.	85.0 g	85 g
4 oz.	113.4 g	125 g
5 oz.	141.7 g	140 g
6 oz.	170.1 g	170 g
7 oz.	198.4 g	200 g
8 oz.	226.8 g	250 g
16 oz.	453.6 g	500 g
32 oz.	907.2 g	1000 g (1 kg)

Casseroles

Canada & Britain		United States	
Standard Size Casserole	Exact Metric Measure	Standard Size Casserole	Exact Metric Measure
1 qt. (5 cups)	1.13 L	1 qt. (4 cups)	900 mL
1 1/2 qts. (7 1/2 cups)	1.69 L	1 1/2 qts. (6 cups)	1.35 L
2 qts. (10 cups)	2.25 L	2 qts. (8 cups)	1.8 L
2 1/2 qts. (12 1/2 cups)	2.81 L	2 1/2 qts. (10 cups)	2.25 L
3 qts. (15 cups)	3.38 L	3 qts. (12 cups)	2.7 L
4 qts. (20 cups)	4.5 L	4 qts. (16 cups)	3.6 L
5 qts. (25 cups)	5.63 L	5 qts. (20 cups)	4.5 L

Tip Index

Recipe Index